CONTENTS

Ships in Focus Publications

Correspondence and editorial:
Roy Fenton
18 Durrington Avenue
London SW20 8NT
020 8879 3527
rfenton@rfenton.demon.co.uk

Orders and photographic:
John & Marion Clarkson
18 Franklands, Longton
Preston PR4 5PD
01772 612855
shipsinfocus@btinternet.com

Printed by Amadeus Press Ltd., Cleckheaton,
Yorkshire.
Designed by Hugh Smallwood, John Clarkson
and Roy Fenton.

SHIPS IN FOCUS RECORD
ISBN 978-1-901703-91-7

SUBSCRIPTION RATES FOR RECORD

Readers can start their subscription with
any issue, and are welcome to backdate it to
receive previous issues.

	3 issues	4 issues
UK	£24	£31
Europe (airmail)	£26	£34
Rest of the world (surface mail)	£26	£34
Rest of the world (airmail)	£31	£41

SHIPS IN FOCUS
March 20

It is with some trepidation that we include in
Graeme Somner's 'Ben Line', which Ships in Focus published about a year
ago. We are, in fact, rather proud of the book: sales have been encouraging
and comments on it have been overwhelmingly favourable. Along with a
personal account from Graeme of his dealings with the company, and his
acknowledgements to those who helped with the book, our follow-up includes
a small number of corrections and additions. The corrections mainly concern
photo captions, and none seriously detract from the information in the book.
Although we aim for zero errors, experience shows that in a book including
over 200 ships, and many thousands of individual pieces of data, there will
be some blunders, despite ourselves and the authors checking the proofs
repeatedly at every stage of production.

Our trepidation arises from the certainty that someone will seize on the
list of corrections and say 'the book contains errors!' This happened with 'Clan
Line: A Fleet History', when an anonymous contributor to a shipping website
claimed it had a serious mistake, but selfishly neglected to tell us, or indeed
anyone, what it was. (We suspect that there was a discrepancy between what
the critic knew, or thought he knew, about the type of engine in a particular Clan
Line ship and what 'Lloyd's Register' published about this engine).

In the end, we would sooner admit to our inadvertent trespasses, and
hope readers forgive them, in the interests of putting the record straight. Indeed,
we would challenge other publishers – several of whom also run magazines
or journals – to do the same and print amendments which come to light after
their books have appeared. And yes, we are thinking of the World Ship Society
here, amongst others. We suspect that few if any shipping books which offer
factual data can be considered absolutely accurate: for evidence, please see the
book reviews in this issue. Errors can sometimes occur because sources like
the vessels registration documents and register books themselves are compiled
by human beings who can and do make errors. In not a few cases allegedly
authoritative sources differ as to the ownership and management details of
ships, a phenomena which has grown much worse over recent decades.

No-one is upset more than we are as editors and publishers by
avoidable mistakes, including the typographical errors which insinuate
themselves into this journal, despite constant vigilance. Needless to say, we
will keep trying to hunt them down. As a traditional song from the north east
of England has it, 'we shall do our best, and the best can do no more'.

John Clarkson   Roy Fenton

March 2010

City of Lichfield: note the bow crest. See page 8. *[W. D. Harris/J. and M.
Clarkson collection]*

ELLERMAN'S CATHEDRAL CITIES

Featuring the eight relatively small motor cargo liners completed for Hall Line and Ellerman and Bucknall between 1957 and 1963, this 'Fleet in Focus' resumes the history of Ellerman group's post-war building programme, begun in 'Record' 21 and continued in 'Record' 27.

Our title 'Cathedral Cities' requires some justification as a city in England, by definition, has to have at least one cathedral. In fact, most of the cities whose names were chosen for this class were better known for their cathedrals than for their urbanisation. These included the county towns of Herefordshire, Gloucestershire, Lancashire, Staffordshire and Worcestershire, plus Lichfield in the English midlands and of Guildford and St. Albans in the south. The only Scottish city originally honoured, Dundee, figured in the list because the ship was built there. As far as is known, this title was not used by Ellerman, who referred to the ships by the names of the lead vessels of the two groups.

Books on Ellerman Lines are silent on the reasons for building these ships, as are contemporary technical journals. At 434 feet overall (405 feet between perpendiculars) they were 50-feet shorter than Ellerman's 'City of Oxford' and 'City of Birkenhead' classes, and dwarfed by the 507-feet 'City of Newcastle' class. Undoubtedly a design consideration was running to the smaller ports in India and Pakistan (and later Bangladesh). However, it is surprising that only three were allocated to Hall Line, who traditionally served India, and the other five to Ellerman and Bucknall who traditionally ran to South Africa. None were registered to City Line, another Ellerman company with roots in the Indian trade. It is significant that the ships of the class were just a little shorter than Liberties. Ellerman had 12 of these, one of the largest groups under the British flag, and sold them off as the 'Cathedral Cities' came into service. Two of the class's names had been previously carried by Liberties, City of Lichfield and City of St. Albans, so it is reasonable to assume they were replacements.

It is dangerous to look for design trends in the diverse Ellerman fleet, as many hands were obviously at work, but these ships seem to have had almost as much in common with the larger Mediterranean traders as their deep-sea predecessors, including just four holds, two ahead and two abaft of the compact superstructure. They were shelter deckers designed to operate in both the open and closed configuration, and had substantial forecastles and poops. The holds were convertible for carrying grain, with a total capacity of around 455,000 cubic feet. Macgregor hatch covers were fitted to three of the holds, the fourth and longest having traditional wooden hatch covers. Four deep tanks just ahead of the engine room could carry vegetable oils, latex or fuel oil. Derricks were of 7- and 10-ton capacity, and provision was made for a 70-ton derrick at the foremast, although photographs show that this was not always carried. Sulzer-type diesels were specified giving a brake horsepower of just over 5,000 at 120 rpm and a service speed of 14¾ knots, although over 16 knots was achieved on trials. Their designed complement was 16 to 17 officers, 37 to 38 ratings, eight or nine catering staff and four cadets. A sign of the times was that no passengers were carried.

The ships were built in two batches, with three beginning with City of Guildford arriving in 1957 and 1958, then an interval until City of St Albans heralded five more delivered from 1960 to 1963. The second batch incorporated some detailed changes, and slightly smaller crew numbers are quoted. The first four of this group entered service as closed shelter deckers, but joined the earlier batch in becoming open shelter deckers within a few years.

In service the ships did trade from Europe to the Indian sub-continent, but also turned up in South and East Africa, in North American ports and in New Zealand. Despite being the last conventional (i.e. engines-amidships) class Ellerman built, they gave comparatively lengthy and largely trouble-free service. The few untoward incidents recorded during their Ellerman careers can be blamed on neither their design nor their crews. Apart from the odd fire in the cargo whilst discharging, the greatest hazard to which one was exposed was the unidentified warship which peppered the City of St Albans during the Pakistan civil war in 1971. All were sold during 1978 and 1979, when the oldest had served Ellerman for 21 years. In contrast to their Ellerman careers, few lasted long under flags of convenience and their further careers were relatively brief and in two cases troubled. None survived more than six years after their sale and, in the case of the former City of Lancaster, actual trading was limited to a matter of months.

CITY OF GUILDFORD (3) 1957-1979

Swan, Hunter and Wigham Richardson Ltd., Wallsend-on-Tyne, 1957; 4,945g, 433 feet

Sulzer-type 8-cyl. 2SCSA oil engine by George Clark and North Eastern Marine (Sunderland) Ltd., Sunderland.

Like most Ellerman ships of the post-war period, City of Guildford was formally owned by Ellerman Lines Ltd. In her case, and of the City of Lancaster and City of Hereford, management was with Hall Line Ltd. of Liverpool and these ships would have flown Hall's house flag. Re-organisation in January 1973 saw subsidiaries including Hall and Ellerman and Bucknall swept away and management transferred to Ellerman City Liners. The photograph of City of Guildford with the maple leaf on her funnel is a rare example of an Ellerman ship not carrying the group's usual funnel markings, and was taken during or shortly after her Canadian service.

After an apparently uneventful but respectable career of 22 years with Ellerman, City of Guildford was sold in 1979. As Eurydice, her new owner was D. Diamantides of Piraeus, who took two other members of the class. Although her post-Ellerman career was relatively short, three names were carried. A 1981 sale saw her renamed Mighty Spirit (final photograph). Her third name, Nirav, was carried only for a final voyage to Bangladesh breakers, arriving at Chittagong in September 1984. *[J. and M. Clarkson collection; J.K. Byass/ World Ship Society Ltd., J. and M. Clarkson; Selim Sam]*

CITY OF LANCASTER (2)
Swan, Hunter and Wigham Richardson Ltd., Wallsend-on-Tyne, 1958; 4,949g, 433 feet
Sulzer-type 8-cyl. 2SCSA oil engine by Sulzer Brothers Ltd., Winterthur, Switzerland.

After 21 years with Ellerman, *City of Lancaster's* further trading career was disastrously short, although her demise was protracted. With her name simply shortened to *Lancaster*, only months after her sale to Diamantides, on 25th September 1979, she collided with the Greek tanker *Thistle Venture* (39,580/1966) in the southern Irish Sea. Her voyage from Calcutta to Glasgow with tea and general cargo sounds very much like she was on charter to Ellerman. *Lancaster* was taken first to Dublin, but for some reason her cargo was not discharged there, and only in March 1980 was she towed to Glasgow to be unloaded. She then languished on the Clyde for over 18 months, until in November 1981 she was towed away to Spain and demolition. *[W.D. Harris/J. and M. Clarkson]*

CITY OF HEREFORD (2)/
CITY OF GLASGOW (5)

Robb Caledon Ltd, Dundee, 1958;
4,954g, 433 feet
Sulzer-type 8-cyl. 2SCSA oil engine by
George Clark and North Eastern Marine
(Sunderland) Ltd., Sunderland

The photograph of City of Hereford at the bottom of the opposite page was taken on trials on 21st November 1958. Note the name pennant at the fore mast: often flown during trials, were these ever flown again during a ship's life?

Differences between the three ships of the first batch were minor. One was the shape of the guard rail around the radar perched on the funnel. This rail appears not to have been fitted in the trials' shot, but is clearly seen in the top photograph on this page.

City of Hereford became *City of Glasgow* (middle and bottom photographs, this page) in 1971, the sole example of a member of the class being renamed whilst in Ellerman ownership. Interestingly, management remained with Hall Line of Liverpool, rather than being transferred to the Glasgow-based City Line, as her new name might have suggested.

On disposal in 1978 she was renamed *Myrna* under the Greek flag. Details were typically complex: nominal owners were the Porter Shipping Company of Liberia, managers Paragon Shipping Co. Ltd. of Piraeus, behind which was one Aristidis E. Ioannidis. He kept her for only two years, however, and in April 1980 *Myrna* sailed from Manila to Kaohsiung for breaking up.
[Roy Fenton collection; Ships in Focus; J.K. Byass/World Ship Society Ltd.; J. and M. Clarkson collection]

CITY OF ST ALBANS (2)

William Denny and Brothers Ltd., Dumbarton, 1960; 7,155g, 434 feet Sulzer-type 8-cyl. 2SCSA oil engine by William Denny and Brothers Ltd, Dumbarton.

First ship of the second batch, *City of St Albans* had a number of detail differences to her superstructure and radar installation. The boat deck was enclosed and a sturdy radar mast fitted on the wheelhouse, rather than having the scanner perched, apparently precariously, on the funnel front. Her initial gross tonnage indicates she was completed as a closed shelter decker, but she was opened up within two years.

She was the member of the class to come closest to disaster whilst with Ellerman and Bucknall. In November 1971, during the civil war that led to the break up of Pakistan, she sailed from Calcutta to Chalna in what was then East Pakistan, following assurances from the authorities in the latter port that all was well. However, when arriving off the Pussur River in the early morning *City of Albans* found herself under fire, and eventually received 49 hits from 40-mm shells. Remarkably, whoever was firing – and suspicion must fall on a Pakistani gunboat – missed everyone on board and failed to hole the ship beneath the waterline.

In 1979 *City of St Albans* went to C.P. Eliopoulos of Piraeus who renamed her *Island of Marmara* (right) under the Greek flag. She was broken up at Jamnagar, India late in 1983.

[Top and bottom; J. and M. Clarkson collection, middle; Roy Fenton collection]

6

CITY OF WORCESTER (2)

Caledon Shipbuilding and Engineering Co. Ltd., Dundee, 1960; 7,149g, 434 feet.

Sulzer-type 8-cyl. 2SCSA oil engine by George Clark and North Eastern Marine (Sunderland) Ltd., Sunderland. City of Worcester was the third member of the class sold to D. Diamantides, who renamed her *Maria* *Diamanto* in 1979. In 1982 he went to the trouble of transferring her from the Greek to the Cyprus flag, which involved registering her under a new owning company and renaming her *Cape Greco*. However, in December of that year she suffered a major machinery failure that required her to finish her voyage from Turkey to Djibouti under tow. A few months later, in August 1983, she ended her days being demolished on Fouzderhat Beach, Chittagong. The two photographs show her with her heavy-lift derrick rigged to handle the heavy cargo carried on her foredeck (top) and with it stowed close to her foremast (bottom) in the Mersey on 31st. August 1968. *[J.K. Byass/World Ship Society Ltd.; J. and M. Clarkson collection]*

CITY OF LICHFIELD (2)
William Denny and Brothers Ltd.,
Dumbarton, 1961; 7,155g, 433 feet
Sulzer-type 8-cyl. 2SCSA oil engine
by William Denny and Brothers Ltd.,
Dumbarton.
As with the first batch, differences
between ships are confined to details
such as the shape of rails round the
radar scanner, although photographs

show these changed over time.
    City of Lichfield, seen above in
South African waters in April 1964, was
another member of the class to have a
very short further trading career after
Ellerman ownership. She was sold in
1978 to Greek owners who hid behind
the anonymity of a Piraeus management
company entitled Richmond Shipping
Co. Ltd. and became simply *Leeds.*

In 1980 a further sale to another
anonymous Greek owner saw her revert
to *City of Leeds.* On 11th November
that year she stranded in a storm during
a voyage from Piraeus to Antalya in
Turkey. Refloated but declared a
constructive total loss, her trading career
had ended, but it took three years before
she was broken up, at Aliaga in Turkey.
[Ships in Focus]

CITY OF DUNDEE (3)
Caledon Shipbuilding and Engineering
Co. Ltd., Dundee, 1961; 7,149g
Sulzer-type 8-cyl. 2SCSA oil engine by
George Clark and North Eastern Marine
(Sunderland) Ltd., Sunderland.
City of Dundee was named in honour of
the city in which she was built. As with

five of the eight ships, management
was with Ellerman and Bucknall, yet
her maiden voyage sounds like it was
on a Hall or City Line service, sailing
for Bombay and Karachi on 20th
June 1961. The photograph at Otago
provides evidence that this class did
trade to New Zealand. The 70-ton

derrick is rigged at her foremast.
In 1978 the same owners who had
taken *City of Leeds* bought her and
renamed her simply *Dundee.* A further
sale in 1980 saw the name *City of
Dundee* restored. She was broken up
at Gadani Beach in early 1984.
[D. Wright]

CITY OF GLOUCESTER (3)

William Denny and Brothers, Dumbarton,
1963; 4,950g, 433 feet
Sulzer-type 8-cyl. 2SCSA oil engine by
William Denny and Brothers, Dumbarton.
The two photographs of *City of
Gloucester*, on the Thames (top) and
sailing from Barry, South Wales (middle),
show her without and with the 70-ton
derrick on her foremast.

With the entire class cleared
out of the fleet in 1978 and 1979, *City of
Gloucester* had the shortest career with
Ellerman, just 16 years. However, she
then spent six years as *Suerte* with C.P.
Eliopoulos (bottom) before being broken
up at Dalian, China in 1985, the last of
the class to survive. *[Ships in Focus; W.
D. Harris/J. and M Clarkson (2)]*

BRITISH SHIPOWNERS' COMPANY LIMITED
Part 1 – The sailing fleet
Malcolm Cooper

The company's formation

The introduction of legislation limiting a shareholder's potential liability to the size of his or her individual shareholding through the passage of the Limited Liability Act of 1855 (18 and 19 VICT c133) produced a virtual tidal wave of ambitious flotations. Many were as grandiose as they were impractical and few passed the test of time. The whole phenomenon left the shipping industry largely untouched. Companies like P&O and Pacific Steam had been formed by royal charter, while other large liner companies like Cunard and Allan were private unlimited partnerships even if they adopted a corporate identity. Most British ships were owned on the long-established 64th share system (effectively an unlimited liability partnership) and were to remain so until the end of the century.

One of the early exceptions to this rule was the British Shipowners' Company Limited. The company was wound up in the early 20th century and has attracted little attention from historians. It had, however, three distinctive characteristics which deserve attention. First, it was a very sizeable limited liability company. Second, it was explicitly established to serve the time charter market and never had a route network of its own. Finally, it maintained this business model through the transition from sail to steam, deliberately building ships for charter to North Atlantic liner operators. While other owners did appear in this business, it was usually on a sporadic single ship basis. British Shipowners' were unique in doing it extensively to the exclusion of all else.

James Beazley, the founder of British Shipowners', was already a significant ship owner in his own right. Born on 4th March 1819 at Gosport, he had come to Liverpool in 1835 at the age of 16 to be apprenticed to the cotton broker Miles Barton. Following completion of his indentures, he had spent some time in South America before returning to Liverpool in 1845 to form his own ship owning business. His initial purchases were largely wooden vessels built in Canada, but he moved to British-built iron sailing ships at the beginning of the 1860s. The heart of his business and the foundations of his fortune were the Australian emigrant trade and the China tea trade. He operated some well-known clippers on both routes – the *Star of the East* and the *Miles Barton* to Australia, and the *Robin Hood* and *Friar Tuck* to China. His last new vessel acquisition was the *Falstaff* of 1875, which remains intact today as a hulk at Punta Arenas. Beazley was obviously a man of some energy as for the bulk of his professional career he managed both his own private fleet and that of British Shipowners' simultaneously. He also benefited from excellent business links within the Liverpool shipping community, whose merchants, builders, brokers and owners would form the bulk of his investors.

The British Shipowners' Co. Ltd. was registered on 30th March 1864. It was a time when the British merchant marine was going through a phase of rapid growth, largely at the expense of the US owners who were selling vessels wholesale as a result of the American Civil War. Perhaps because of this, Beazley set himself a hopelessly ambitious nominal share capital target of £2,000,000, divided into 100,000 shares of £200 each. When one considers that the average price of a new 1,200-ton iron fully-rigged ship was approximately £15,000, this means that Beazley could have been aiming for a fleet of over 100 vessels! Some degree of sanity was introduced in 1868 when the nominal capital was reduced to £1,000,000, but by then only £375,000 had actually been raised, and the company's real capital was never to be greatly in excess of £500,000. Even these sums, however, were sufficient to fund a fleet of 20 ships, and, up to the end of the 1870s, British Shipowners' controlled one of the largest sail fleets on the UK register.

James Beazley was the largest single shareholder in the company until his retirement. His initial investment was £11,250, and the family's stake would build up to roughly double that towards the end of the company's life. The list of other large shareholders reads like a 'Who's Who' of the Liverpool shipping community: Joseph Hubback 1,800 shares, Samuel Graves 1,000 shares, Thomas Horsfall 1,000 shares, George Clover 400 shares, and others. There were a few outsiders, most notably John Elder, the Glasgow shipbuilder, and James Nicol Fleming, the as-yet not disgraced Glasgow banker, but the company was very much a Liverpool venture built on the foundations of Beazley's business associates.

Early expansion

Beazley got the company off the ground by selling it two of his own ships (in reality he almost certainly took shares as part of his compensation). One of these was the two-year-old *Nelson* bought second hand from Lewis and Alexander Potter of Glasgow. The other was the brand new *Glenna*, which Beazley purchased from her Liverpool owners two weeks after her initial registration. The departure of the *Glenna* on her maiden voyage coincided almost to the day with the company's formation. It was not to prove a happy coincidence. The formalities of sale were not completed for a further two months, and by that time the vessel may already have gone down. One way or the other, she was never seen again and her register was finally closed in July 1865.

The company's own acquisition programme got off to a roaring start, with two other ships joining the fleet in 1864 and five in 1865. Six of the seven were new vessels built for the company, and one was an almost new ship. All were given names beginning *British*, establishing a nomenclature which the company was to employ with only isolated exceptions throughout its life. The 1864 arrivals were *British Prince* and *British Sovereign*; while the 1865 additions were *British Princess, British Nation, British*

Monarch, British Peer and *British Viceroy* (ex-*Glenburnie*). It is striking that while three of the new ships came from one builder, G.R. Clover of Birkenhead (a shareholder in the company), the others all came from separate yards – all of them in Ireland. The iron sailing ship was still a relative novelty in the mid-1860s, and the company would not have a large number of builders from whom to invite tenders.

Expansion continued through the second half of the decade, but henceforth British Shipowners' were able to depend on Merseyside yards, particular those of Royden and Vernon. 1866 saw the arrival of *British Envoy, British Flag* and *British Consul*. Three more vessels followed in 1867: *British Admiral, British Statesman* and *British India* (ex-*Sorabjee Jamsetjee Jeejeebhoy*). After this the pace of growth slowed, with only one new ship in each of 1868, *British Sceptre*, and 1869, *British Navy*.

Beyond the missing *Glenna*, the company had been fortunate enough to escape any maritime losses, so the British Shipowners' fleet was 16-strong when it entered the 1870s. This was close to the maximum that its available capital would allow, and henceforth new additions would be more or less balanced by casualties. The company was nonetheless now one of the largest owners of iron sail tonnage in the country. Its vessels were largely employed in the Indian, Far Eastern and Australian trades, businesses in which Beazley had already established a strong network of business contacts.

Mixed fortunes in the 1870s

The 1870s were to prove a decade of mixed fortunes for the firm's sailing fleet. Two vessels entered the fleet in 1870, the newly-built *British King* and the second-hand *British Commodore* (ex-*Knight Bachelor*). The year 1872, however, was to see severe setbacks: the *British Prince* was wrecked on the Bass Rock while still in the charge of a pilot, and the *British Flag* and *British Admiral* were lost at sea. The company made good its losses in the following year. The *British Ambassador* arrived new from her builders, and was joined by two second-hand acquisitions, *The Bruce* and the *Lady Cairns*. For some reason the firm abandoned its normal practice, renaming neither of the pair.

In 1874, the firm sold the *British Monarch* to another Liverpool owner. As the vessel was only 10 years old, and there were to be no further disposals before 1880, the suspicion must be that she was deemed in some way unsatisfactory. Either that, or there was a need to quickly raise some extra capital for new building, as the same year saw the delivery of three more new vessels: *British Admiral* (2), *British General* and *British Commerce*. Unfortunately the new *British Admiral* was destined to become the firm's most disastrous maritime casualty. Nearing the end of her maiden voyage to Melbourne, she was wrecked on a reef two miles off the south west coast of King's Island. She was carrying passengers as well as the normal general cargo, and fatalities were heavy. Only nine of the 88 aboard made it safely to shore.

Most of British Shipowners' vessels belonged to the class of iron clippers of the 1860s and 1870s, with the years 1873 and 1874 perhaps representing their zenith. The *British Ambassador* of 1873 was the fastest of the fleet - in Basil Lubbock's words 'a vessel with the cut away lines of a modern yacht and the holder of the record between San Francisco and Australia'. This 'record" was for an iron ship: the *Ambassador* went from San Francisco to Newcastle, NSW, in 38 days in 1888. *[John Naylon collection]*

After a decade of rapid expansion and a short rash of losses, the second half of the 1870s proved something of an anticlimax. The *British Viceroy* was lost in the Hooghly in 1875, and the *British King* went missing in the following year. Only two new vessels joined the fleet, the *British Duke* in 1875 and the *British Enterprise* in 1876. In addition, two of the older and smaller members of the fleet, the *British Princess* and the *British Peer,* were each lengthened by some 30 feet. For a firm that had demonstrated so much early dynamism, such relative inactivity might seem to have indicated a loss of direction. There are a number of reasons to suggest that nothing of the sort was true.

As far as the firm itself was concerned, the available capital must have been close to fully invested. While no financial statements have come to hand, there is no reason to doubt that it was prospering. While the Far East trade was in decline, contraction there was more than balanced by the rapid growth of commerce between the UK and India. The Australian trade was on a long upward curve. Emigrants provided a steady source of revenue while, on the cargo side, the growing colonial economy's need for western manufactured goods was complemented by Australia's own rising output of primary goods such as wool and grain. In addition, freight rates had yet to enter the long move downwards which would commence in the last decades of the century, and cyclicality was relatively muted. Beazley was a very experienced ship manager, and it seems all but certain that he and his staff had few serious problems in keeping the company's ships busy in the charter market.

Beyond these business fundamentals, there is also a strong technological element to the story. There were no significant changes in sailing ship design (beyond a short dalliance with composite construction) between 1850s and the 1880s. Things only began to change when steel replaced iron in the early 1880s, and when carrying capacity began to outweigh speed towards the end of the same decade. In brief, an iron sailing ship of 1,200-1,500 tons was as competitive a proposition in 1880 as in 1860. In addition, the average physical and economic life of an iron sailing vessel was far longer than its more expensive and more fragile steam equivalent. The latter would require serious attention to its power plant after about a decade, and would be struggling to pass its third survey without a fairly comprehensive overhaul. While some vessels certainly lasted longer, the average life of a steamer was about 20 years. The equivalent figure for an iron sailing vessel was some 50% longer. Indeed, there were very few cases of iron sailing ships being hulked or broken up before the 1890s. Those that did not succumb to weather or navigational hazard could and would just keep sailing, with the only factors bearing down on operating costs being fairly regular replacement of damaged sails or rigging, and the relatively inexpensive refitting of masts or decking.

Most of the factors described above were common to the whole British iron sail fleet. The only factor that was peculiar to British Shipowners' up to the late 1870s was its structure as a limited liability company with a single capital base – most other ships were owned and financed as separate 64th share ventures. A dramatic change took place, however, around the time the *British Enterprise* joined the fleet – the company decided to invest in steam tonnage and to try its built-for-charter business model in a bold, and risky move into the North Atlantic passenger trade.

This new venture will be described in the second part of this history. Here we will concentrate only on the further history of the sailing fleet. While the firm would reduce the scale of sail operations and divert the bulk of its capital into steam, it did not finally abandon the older

Harland and Wolff gave the *British Merchant* the same sail plan as the better-known jute clippers *Slieve More* and *Slieve Bawn*. On her maiden voyage the *British Merchant* went out to Melbourne from Liverpool in 77 days; in 1883 she came home from San Francisco to the Tuskar in 89 days; and in 1887 she made the Hooghly from Liverpool in 79 days. *[John Naylon collection]*

technology for a full two decades, and would even build a handful of new sailing vessels after its steamers entered service.

The swansong of sail

British Shipowners' entered the 1880s with a 20-strong sailing fleet. Two steamers had already entered service and contracts had been signed for a further two steamers and a pair of new sailing vessels with the expanded deadweight capacity necessary to meet the changing demands of the charter market. The company had already called up fresh capital from its existing shareholders, but more was needed. It thus had a choice of diluting existing shareholdings by seeking further capital from outside the existing share register or raising funds through asset disposals. The managers took the second option – almost certainly to ensure that they retained a significant shareholding in the business.

Five sailing vessels were sold in 1880, and another five in 1881. There were two further disposals in 1882 before the retrenchment programme was brought to an end by three final sales in 1883. In the latter year, the sail fleet was further reduced when the *British Enterprise* was abandoned to the underwriters after sinking in the Tyne (she would subsequently be raised and enjoy a long second career with another owner). The buyers of sold-off ships were all Liverpool or London ship owners, many of whom were in the early stages of building up their own fleets. Leyland Brothers, Gillison and Chadwick and Sandbach, Tinne and Co, all of Liverpool, each acquired a pair. So too did James Nourse of London. In what can only be described as a cruel twist of fate, two vessels were lost almost before the ink had dried on their bills of sale. The *British Navy* dragged her anchors in the Downs while riding out a storm, drove down on another vessel and foundered. The *British Commerce* sank following a collision with another sailing vessel in the English Channel.

Perhaps the most significant of the vessel sales was that of the *British Princess* to Gracie, Beazley and Co. in 1883. Edward Beazley was one of James's Beazley's sons, and was involved with British Shipowners' as a shareholder. Like his father before him, however, he also carried out shipping business outside the firm. In 1882 he went into a partnership with William Gracie which was established to purchase the sailing fleet of the Liverpool millers J. Heap and Sons, which was subsequently managed as the Australasian Shipping Co. Ltd. Gracie, Beazley and Co. would eventually become the last managers of British Shipowners' and would run the business for the last decade of its existence.

The large-scale retrenchment of the early 1880s left only five of the original fleet in company ownership: *British Sceptre* (1868), *British Ambassador* (1873), *British General* (1874), *British Duke* (1875) and the *British Enterprise* (1876). Of these, the last two were lost before the decade was out; the former wrecked in 1888, and the latter abandoned to the underwriters in 1883 as already explained. However, whilst the company had considerably reduced its commitment to sail, there was no question of it leaving the business altogether. Two new ships arrived in 1880: the *British Yeoman* from Oswald, Mordaunt and Co. of Southampton, and the *British Merchant* from Harland and Wolff, who were actually building a steamer for the company on an adjacent berth. There was one last addition to the sailing fleet. In 1884, John Reid and Co. of Port Glasgow delivered the *British Isles*. Fittingly enough, she was, at just under 2,500 tons gross register, easily the largest sailing ship the company ever owned.

The *British Yeoman*, although launched in the same month and year as the *British Merchant* (August 1880), illustrates the transition from the clipper models of her predecessors to the carrier models to come - as well as the distinct concepts of the two builders, Harland and Wolff and Oswald, Mordaunt. *[John Naylon collection]*

The final years

Commercial logic may have brought an end to investment in sail, as the steamship began to make serious inroads into the long-distance bulk trades following the arrival of steel construction and the triple-expansion steam engine in the early 1880s. It may also have had something to do with the arrival of a new generation at the head of the managing company. In late 1885 James Beazley retired at the age of 66 after a long and busy career. He was succeeded as manager by one of his sons, James Henry Beazley, on the 3rd of December of that year.

J.H. Beazley stayed at the helm of British Shipowners' for a decade. The residual sailing fleet remained intact until the aged *British Sceptre* was sold to A.D. Bordes of Dunkirk in December 1891. In an eerie repeat of earlier losses, she lasted less than a month under French colours, going aground off the Dutch coast before the month was out. All but one of the remaining sailing ships were sold in the middle of the decade: the *British Ambassador* to a German owner in 1894, the *British Merchant* to another German in 1895, and the *British General* and *British Yeoman* to British companies in 1896 (see 'Record' 41 for an account of the long and chequered subsequent career of the *British Yeoman*). The *British Isles* soldiered on alone until 1899 when she was sold to another Liverpool shipping concern.

In the midst of this disposal process, British Shipowners' experienced its third and final change of management. On 9th July 1895, Gracie, Beazley and Co., now a well established shipping business, took over from J.H. Beazley, management itself being formally vested in Edwin Arthur Beazley. Thus the company was to be a Beazley family concern throughout its life. From the late 1870s its fortunes had been tied to steam and the North Atlantic passenger trade. This separate chapter of the British Shipowners' story will be covered in a second article. Before leaving the story of sail, it is worth dwelling on one point. The company's steam fleet was sold in 1906 and the company itself sold soon after. At that time, at least half a dozen of its former sailing ships were still serving their new owners. The most durable was to prove the *British Ambassador* which traded for eight years as a Portuguese auxiliary schooner before being broken up in 1928. At that time, only one of the steamers built for the company between 1878 and 1901 was still afloat. *[To be continued]*

Fleet list part 1: sailing ships

All vessels were iron, three-masted and ship-rigged apart from the steel *British Isles*.

1. GLENNA 1864-1865
O.N. 48791   1,282g 1,282n
213.0 x 36.8 x 22.4 feet
1864: Launched at West Hartlepool.
2.3.1864: Registered at Liverpool (86/1864) in the ownership of William Pirrie and Robert Reid as GLENNA.
18.3.1864: Sold to James Beazley and Son, Liverpool.
21.3.1864: Re-registered at Liverpool (116/1864) in the name of James Beazley.
3.1864: Sailed from Sunderland for China and went missing.
17.5.1864: Acquired by British Shipowners' Co. Ltd., Liverpool.
27.7.1865: Register closed.

2. NELSON 1864-1880
O.N. 44774   1,248g 1,248n
214.4 x 36.2 x 22.9 feet
8.4.1862: Launched by Laurence Hill and Co., Port Glasgow for Potter, Wilson and Co., Glasgow as NELSON.
16.4.1862: Registered at Glasgow (44/1862) in the ownership of Lewis and Alexander Potter, William Birrell and William Orr.
1864: Sold to James Beazley and Son, Liverpool.
1.9.1864: Acquired by British Shipowners' Co. Ltd., Liverpool.
5.9.1864: Registered at Liverpool (371/1864) in the name of James Beazley (sale to British Shipowners' not registered until after Liverpool registration).
11.5.1880: Sold (48/64 shares) to R.W. Leyland and Co., Liverpool.
16.10.1880: Residual 16 shares sold to same owner.
24.10.1882: Foundered after being abandoned about 16 miles east by north of the North Hinder Light Vessel while on a voyage from South Shields to Valparaiso with a cargo of coal. All 23 members of the crew were rescued.
14.11.1882: Register closed.

3. BRITISH PRINCE (1) 1864-1872
O.N. 51008   1,210g 1,210n
208.4 x 36.2 x 22.8 feet
17.9.1864: Launched by G.R. Clover and Co., Birkenhead (Yard No.7).
24.10.1864: Registered at Liverpool (446/1864) in the ownership of British Shipowners' Co. Ltd., Liverpool as BRITISH PRINCE.
3.2.1872: Wrecked near the Bass Rock whilst on a voyage from Dundee to Calcutta.
13.3.1872: Register closed.

4. BRITISH SOVEREIGN 1864-1880
O.N. 51030   1,345g 1,292n
213.2 x 34.2 x 22.8 feet
10.1864: Launched by Robinson, Cork.
30.11.1864: Registered at Liverpool (489/1864) in the ownership of British Shipowners' Co. Ltd., Liverpool as BRITISH SOVEREIGN.
30.3.1880: Sold (48/64 shares) to Gillison and Chadwick, Liverpool.
14.10.1880: Residual 16 shares sold to same owner.
24.4.1881: Sailed from Dundee for San Francisco with a cargo of coal and went missing with her crew of 23.
24.12.1881: Register closed.
28.12.1881: Posted missing at Lloyd's.

5. BRITISH PRINCESS (1) 1865-1883
O.N. 51435   1,283g 1,283n
212.7 x 36.1 x 23.0 feet
1875: 1,543g 1,480n
246.7 x 36.7 x 22.8 feet
28.1.1865: Launched by G.R. Clover and Co., Birkenhead (Yard No.8).
23.2.1865: Registered at Liverpool (60/1865) in the ownership of British Shipowners' Co. Ltd., Liverpool as BRITISH PRINCESS.
15.2.1871: Re-registered at Liverpool (24/1871) after re-measurement.
20.10.1875: Re-registered at Liverpool (172/1875) after lengthening.
10.3.1883: Sold to Gracie, Beazley and Co., Liverpool and reduced to a barque.
6.1900: Sold to C.J. Klingenberg and Co., Bremen, Germany and renamed LOUISE.
27.6.1900: Register closed.
2.1907: Broken up at Genoa.

6. BRITISH PEER 1865-1883
O.N. 51452   1,230g 1,230n
218.0 x 36.2 x 22.9 feet
1878: 1,478g 1,428n
247.5 x 36.5 x 22.5 feet
31.1.1865: Launched by Harland and Wolff, Belfast (Yard No.32).
20.3.1865: Registered at Liverpool (89/1865) in the ownership of British Shipowners' Co. Ltd., Liverpool as BRITISH PEER.
19.8.1878: Re-registered at Liverpool (107/1878) after lengthening.
14.3.1883: Sold to James Nourse, London.
16.3.1883: Re-registered at London (48/1883) in the name of James Nourse.
8.12.1896: Wrecked in Saldanha Bay while on a voyage from London to Cape Town with general cargo. Of her crew, 14 were lost.
8.1.1897: Register closed.

7. BRITISH NATION 1865-1880
O.N. 51477   1,302g 1,302n
216.2 x 35.3 x 22.9 feet
3.1865: Launched by Walpole, Webb and Bewley, Dublin.
27.4.1865: Registered at Liverpool

The *British Peer* was reckoned to be the fastest ship in the British Shipowners' fleet until the advent of the *British Ambassador,* Her owners sought to solve the problem of the ever-increasing size of ships by lengthening the *British Peer* and *British Princess,* both built in 1865. The *British Peer* was lengthened in 1878, raising her tonnage from 1,230 to 1,428, but this spoilt her sailing qualities. She is seen here wrecked in Saldanha Bay in 1896, while under James Nourse's ownership. *[John Naylon collection]*

(133/1865) in the ownership of British Shipowners' Co. Ltd., Liverpool as BRITISH NATION.
2.4.1880: Sold to Sandbach, Tinne and Co., Liverpool.
4.1888: Sold to C. Henoch junior (J.C. Pluger and Co., managers), Bremen, Germany and renamed H. HACKFELD.
24.4.1888: Register closed.
1902: Sold to Acties. Australia (J. Johansen and Co., managers), Christiana, Norway and renamed AUSTRALIA.
1909: Deleted from 'Lloyd's Register'.

8. BRITISH MONARCH 1865-1874
O.N. 51482 1,262g 1,262n
212.1 x 36.4 x 23.2 feet
27.4.1865: Launched by G.R. Clover and Co., Birkenhead (Yard No.9).
6.5.1865: Registered at Liverpool (143/1865) in the ownership of British Shipowners' Co. Ltd., Liverpool as BRITISH MONARCH.
31.12.1874: Sold to H. Fernie and Sons, Liverpool.
1.1880: Reduced to a barque.
29.11.1889: Abandoned on fire off South Africa.
6.1.1890: Register closed.

9. BRITISH VICEROY 1865-1875
O.N. 50380 1,173g 1,173n
214.4 x 34.9 x 22.0 feet
12.1864: Launched by the Union Steam Boat Co., Kelvinhaugh, Glasgow.
4.2.1865: Registered at Glasgow (16/1865) in the ownership of David Davidson, George Robertson Andrews, John Wood and Francis Neilson as GLENBURNIE.
17.5.1865: Sold to Wilson and Co., Liverpool and re-sold to British Shipowners' Co. Ltd., being 'sold foreign' in the process to facilitate name change.

18.5.1865: Re-registered at Liverpool (155/1865) in the name of the company as BRITISH VICEROY.
31.8.1875: Lost in the Hooghly River.
9.11.1875: Register closed.

10. BRITISH ENVOY 1866-1881
O.N. 54969 1,265g 1,265n
214.5 x 35.9 x 22.9 feet
4.1866: Launched by Thomas Royden and Sons, Liverpool (Yard No.89).
29.5.1866: Registered at Liverpool (135/1866) in the ownership of British Shipowners' Co. Ltd., Liverpool as BRITISH ENVOY.
9.5.1881: Sold to John Coupland and Co., Liverpool and subsequently reduced to a barque.
3.6.1889: Taken over by mortgagees, William David Lloyd and Henry William Lowe, London.
8.1891: Sold for £5,500 to Carl August Banck, Helsingborg, Sweden.
7.8.1891: Register closed.
1901: Sold to Acties. Arabia (J. Johansen and Co., managers), Christiana, Norway and renamed ARABIA.
9.8.1909: Driven ashore and wrecked whilst loading at Cape Chatte after a ballast voyage from Buenos Aires.

11. BRITISH FLAG 1866-1872
O.N. 55007 1,285g 1,285n
218.5 x 36.4 x 22.9 feet
7.1866: Launched by Thomas Vernon and Son, Seacombe for British Shipowners' Co. Ltd., Liverpool as BRITISH FLAG.
29.8.1866: Registered at Liverpool (211/1866) in the ownership of British Shipowners' Co. Ltd., Liverpool as BRITISH FLAG.
11.1872: Lost at sea.
5.4.1873: Register closed

12. BRITISH CONSUL 1866-1881
O.N. 55001 1,267g 1,267n
214.9 x 36.0 x 22.6 feet
8.1866: Launched by Thomas Royden and Sons, Liverpool (Yard No.90).
7.9.1866: Registered at Liverpool (217/1866) in the ownership of British Shipowners' Co. Ltd., Liverpool as BRITISH CONSUL.
26.10.1881: Sold to Trinder, Anderson and Co., London.
2.3.1883: Renamed MORIALTA and re-registered at London (34/1883).
9.1898: Sold to Skibsacties. Tercia (Bendix J. Grefstad, manager), Grimstad, Norway and renamed TERCIA.
11.3.1908: Wrecked near Vergennes while on a voyage from Hernosand to Punta Arenas with a cargo of cement and timber.

13. BRITISH ADMIRAL (1) 1867-1872
O.N. 55071 1,269g 1,269n
218.5 x 36.4 x 22.9 feet
2.1867: Launched by Thomas Vernon and Son, Seacombe.
28.3.1867: Registered at Liverpool (87/1867) in the ownership of British Shipowners' Co. Ltd., Liverpool as BRITISH ADMIRAL.
14.1.1872: Abandoned in the China Sea.
15.4.1872: Register closed.

14. BRITISH STATESMAN 1867-1880
O.N. 55087 1,262g 1,262n
217.0 x 36.0 x 22.8 feet
4.1867: Launched by Thomas Royden and Sons, Liverpool (Yard No.92).
14.5.1867: Registered at Liverpool (138/1867) in the ownership of British Shipowners' Co. Ltd., Liverpool as BRITISH STATESMAN.
10.6.1880: Sold to Sandbach, Tinne and Co., Liverpool.
17.8.1885: Foundered at the Sandheads, Bay of Bengal.
23.9.1865: Register closed.

15. BRITISH INDIA 1867-1881
O.N. 51433 1,199g 1,119n
207.2 x 35.2 x 22.2 feet
31.12.1864: Launched by Laird Brothers, Birkenhead (Yard No.314) for James Parsons, Liverpool, acting on behalf of the Union Shipping Co. Ltd., Bombay as SORABJEE JAMSETJEE JEEJEEBHOY.
14.2.1865: Registered at Liverpool (52/1865) in the name of James Parsons.
26.10.1865: Re-registered at Bombay (18/1865) in the name of the Union Shipping Co. Ltd., Bombay.
31.8.1867: Acquired by British Shipowners' Co. Ltd., Liverpool.
6.9.1867: Re-registered at Liverpool (229/1867) and immediately 'sold foreign' to facilitate name change.
12.9.1867: Re-registered at Liverpool (242/1867) in the ownership of the company as BRITISH INDIA.
1.6.1881: Sold (48 shares) to R.W. Leyland and Co., Liverpool.

23.12.1881: Residual 16 shares sold to same owner.
19.1.1894: Abandoned on fire 30 miles north west of Madeira in position 33.10 north by 17.30 west while on a voyage from Leith to Rio de Janeiro with a cargo of gas coal; sank the following day.
1.2.1894: Register closed.

16. BRITISH SCEPTRE 1868-1891
O.N. 60066 1,484g 1,436n
224.3 x 37.8 x 23.5 feet
22.4.1868: Launched by Thomas Royden and Sons, Liverpool (Yard No.104).
27.5.1868: Registered at Liverpool (93/1868) in the ownership of British Shipowners' Co. Ltd., Liverpool as BRITISH SCEPTRE.
12.1891: Sold to Ant. Dom. Bordes et fils, Dunkirk, France and renamed IQUIQUE.
12.12.1891: Register closed.
30.12.1891: Wrecked on Ooster Bank, near Brouwershaven, whilst on a voyage from Newcastle-upon-Tyne to Valparaiso with a cargo of coal.

17. BRITISH NAVY 1869-1881
O.N. 58963 1,263g 1,217n
206.0 x 35.5 x 23.2 feet
1.1869: Launched by the Liverpool Shipbuilding Co. Ltd., Liverpool for British Shipowners' Co. Ltd.
23.1.1869: Registered at Liverpool (16/1869) in the ownership of British Shipowners' Co. Ltd., Liverpool as BRITISH NAVY.
15.11.1881: Sold to J. Boumphrey and Co., Liverpool.
26.11.1881: Dragged anchor while riding out a storm in the Downs on a voyage from London to Sydney. New South Wales with general cargo; drove down on the anchored British iron sailing vessel LARNACA (1,497/1878) and foundered on Cinders Bank near the South Foreland. The crew was saved.
22.12.1881: Register closed.

18. BRITISH COMMODORE 1870-1882
O.N. 56924 1,453g 1,390n
221.6 x 36.1 x 24.7 feet
22.2.1868: Launched by Palmers' Shipbuilding and Iron Co. Ltd., Jarrow (Yard No.224) for Carlyle and Co., London as KNIGHT COMMANDER.
26.2.1868: Registered at London (44/1868) in the ownership of James and Robert Carlyle.
10.1870: Acquired by British Shipowners' Co. Ltd., Liverpool.
22.10.1870: Re-registered at Liverpool (189/1870) in the ownership of British Shipowners' Co. Ltd., Liverpool as BRITISH COMMODORE.
4.5.1882 to 5.10.1882: Sold to Samuel Parry and Robert H. Jones, Liverpool.
19.3.1890: Robert H. Jones becomes sole managing owner.
23.3.1893: Sold for £8,960 to British Commodore Ltd. (Robert H. Jones, manager), Liverpool.

10.6.1898: Sold to Sir Edward James Reed KCB (naval constructor acting as an agent for the Chilean Navy).
7.1898: Sold to the Chilean Government through the Chilean Vice-Consul at Cardiff.
18.7.1898: Sailed from Barry Docks for Punta Arenas.
2.11.1898: Formally handed over to her new owners at Punta Arenas; subsequently reduced to a coal hulk in the same port.
14.12.1898: Register closed.

19. BRITISH ARMY 1872-1882
O.N. 62332 1,338g 1,289n
221.1 x 36.9 x 22.7 feet
9.1869: Launched by T.R. Oswald and Co., Sunderland (Yard No.83) for Middle Dock Co., Sunderland as CYNRIC.
23.10.1869: Registered at Sunderland (63/1869) in the ownership of Thomas Hood Henderson and John Anthony Woods.
1.3.1872: Acquired by British Shipowners' Co. Ltd., Liverpool.
23.3.1872: Renamed BRITISH ARMY.
1.4.1872: Re-registered at Liverpool (45/1872) still in the names of the original owners; sale to the company and formal change of ownership effected later the same day.
25.3.1882 to 26.9.1882: Sold to Gillison and Chadwick, Liverpool.
6.6.1896: Dismasted in a gale in the South Atlantic in position 54.30 south by 62.00 west while on a voyage from Barry Docks to Pisagua with a cargo of coal; put back to Rio de Janeiro.
14.9.1896: Condemned as a constructive total loss at Rio de Janeiro.
26.10.1896: Sold to Wilson, Sons and Co., Rio de Janeiro for use as a hulk.
27.4.1897: Register closed.

20. BRITISH KING (1) 1872-1877
O.N. 63230 1,656g 1,581n
246.1 x 40.3 x 23.8 feet
11.1869: Launched by Thomas Royden and Sons, Liverpool (Yard No.121).
25.1.1870: Registered at Liverpool (5/1870) in the ownership of Carruthers C. Johnson (20/64), Thomas Comber (16/64), Thomas B. Royden (16/64), Joseph Lyne (4/64), Jonathon Jenkinson (4/64) and Edward Caird (4/64) trading as S. Johnson and Co. as GLEN SANNOX.
25.4.1872: Acquired by British Shipowners' Co. Ltd., Liverpool and renamed BRITISH KING.
9.5.1872: Re-registered at Liverpool (62/1872).
30.5.1876: Sailed from Newcastle-upon-Tyne for San Francisco, USA with a cargo of coal and went missing.
8.2.1877: Register closed.
14.2.1877: Posted missing at Lloyd's.

21. LADY CAIRNS 1873-1881
O.N. 60323 1,311g 1,265n
216.4 x 35.4 x 22.5 feet
24.4.1869: Launched by Harland and Wolff, Belfast (Yard No.60) for their own account.

1869: Registered at Belfast in the ownership of Edward J. Harland and Gustav W. Wolff as LADY CAIRNS.
10.1.1873: Re-registered at Liverpool (4/1873).
8.2.1873: Acquired by British Shipowners' Co. Ltd., Liverpool.
29.12.1881: Sold to Richard Martin and Co., Dublin.
5.1.1882: Re-registered at Dublin (1/1882).
10.1890: Sold to Lawrence Tulloch, Swansea.
5.11.1890: Re-registered at Swansea (13/1890).
20.3.1904: Sunk in collision with the iron barque MONA (1,096/1878) in the Irish Sea about 25 miles west of the Kish Lightship off Queenstown while on a voyage to Timaru, New Zealand. The entire crew of 22 was lost.

22. BRITISH AMBASSADOR 1873-1894
O.N. 69308 1,864g 1,794n
262.0 x 41.9 x 23.9 feet
8.1873: Launched by Potter, Hodgkinson and Co., Liverpool (Yard No.45).
17.10.1873: Registered at Liverpool (169/1873) in the ownership of British Shipowners' Co. Ltd., Liverpool as BRITISH AMBASSADOR.
2.3.1894: Sold at Hamburg to E.C. Schramm and Co., Bremen, Germany and renamed EMILIE.
27.3.1894: Register closed.
10.12.1909: Sold to August Bolten, Wm. Miller's Nachfolger, Hamburg, Germany.
10.1910: Sold to Da Costa Vaques, Lisbon, Portugal.
1920: Sold to A. Marittima Soc. Anon. de Responsibilidade Ltda., Lisbon, converted to a two-masted auxiliary motor schooner and renamed DABEJA.
6.1928: Sold for £2,300 to be broken up.

23. BRITISH ADMIRAL (2) 1874
O.N. 69329 1,808g 1,744n
257.6 x 41.9 x 23.9 feet
11.1873: Launched by Thomas Royden and Sons, Liverpool (Yard No.157).
2.1.1874: Registered at Liverpool (2/1874) in the ownership of British Shipowners' Co. Ltd., Liverpool as BRITISH ADMIRAL.
23.5.1874: Wrecked on a reef two miles off the south west coast of King's Island, Tasmania, between Currie Harbour and the Ettrick River while on a voyage from Liverpool to Melbourne with general cargo and 49 passengers. Of the 88 on board, 79 were drowned and nine saved.
12.8.1874: Register closed.

24. THE BRUCE 1874-1880
O.N. 55027 1,200g 1,146n
224.2 x 35.6 x 22.3 feet
9.10.1866: Launched by Aitken and Mansell, Whiteinch, Glasgow (Yard No.17).
23.11.1866: Registered at Liverpool (283/1866) in the ownership of W. and R. Wright, Liverpool as THE BRUCE.

17.3.1873: Acquired by British Shipowners' Co. Ltd., Liverpool.
12.5.1874: Re-registered at Liverpool (72/1874).
8.7.1880: Sold to James Nourse, London.
13.7.1880: Re-registered at London (73/1880).
1889: Reduced to a barque.
18.2.1891: Capsized in New York harbour and abandoned to the underwriters. Later salved and reduced to a coal hulk.
14.4.1891: Register closed.
1898: Returned to service as the schooner barge WEST POINT owned by Lewis Luckenbach, New York.
1903: Transferred to Luckenbach Transport and Wrecking Co., New York.
1908: Transferred to the estate of Lewis Luckenbach.
1910: Transferred to Edgar F. Luckenbach, New York.
1921: Sold to Neptune Lines Inc., New York.
1930: Sold to Durham Navigation Corporation, New York.
1931: Resold to Neptune Lines Inc., New York.
1934: Dismantled.

25. BRITISH GENERAL 1874-1896
O.N. 69366 1,810g 1,754n
257.6 x 41.9 x 23.9 feet
4.1874: Launched by Thomas Royden and Sons, Liverpool (Yard No.158).
25.5.1874: Registered at Liverpool (83/1874) in the ownership of British Shipowners' Co. Ltd., Liverpool as BRITISH GENERAL.
17.2.1896: Sold to Thomas Roberts, Llanelly.
22.2.1896: Re-registered at Llanelly (1/1896).
30.3.1902: Ownership transferred to David T. Roberts and Annie Roberts following the death of Thomas Roberts.
25.8.1902: Register closed on sale to Glama and Marinho, Oporto, Portugal and renamed EUROPA.
1908: Reduced to a hulk.

26. BRITISH COMMERCE 1874-1883
O.N. 70888 1,463g 1,417n
246.2 x 37.3 x 21.4 feet
7.11.1874: Launched by Dobie and Co., Govan, Glasgow (Yard No.72).
5.12.1874: Registered at Liverpool (185/1874) in the ownership of British Shipowners' Co. Ltd., Liverpool as BRITISH COMMERCE.
30.3.1883: Sold to William Thomas and Co., Liverpool.
25.4.1883: Foundered after a collision with the British iron sailing ship COUNTY OF ABERDEEN (1,943/1879) in the English Channel, 16 miles south of the Owers Lightship in position 50.22 north by 00.36 west while on a voyage from London to Melbourne with general cargo. Of the 27 on board, 24 were lost (including two stowaways) and three saved.
2.5.1883: Register closed.

The *British General* was a sister ship of the *British Admiral* and was equally heavily sparred, with a main yard 96 feet long. After the tragic loss of the *Admiral,* the *British General's* spars were reduced, which probably accounts for her not being known for any record passages. She is seen above towing up to Bristol with her main skysail yard sent down and jib boom run in; this was later replaced by a spike bowsprit, as seen below. *[Both: John Naylon collection]*

27. BRITISH DUKE 1875-1888
O.N. 70904 1,464g 1,420n
232.8 x 38.0 x 23.5 feet
21.1.1875: Launched by Barrow Shipbuilding Co. Ltd., Barrow (Yard No.19).
12.2.1875: Registered at Liverpool (18/1875) in the ownership of British Shipowners' Co. Ltd., Liverpool as BRITISH DUKE.
13.11.1888: Wrecked 1½ miles west of Klippen Point, Cape Francis, Cape of Good Hope in position 34.11 south by 24.35 east while on a voyage from Calcutta to London with general cargo.
20.12.1888: Register closed.

28. BRITISH ENTERPRISE 1876-1883
O.N. 76369 1,696g 1,640n
246.0 x 40.1 x 23.9 feet
5.10.1876: Launched by Richardson, Duck

and Co., Stockton-on-Tees (Yard No.222).
18.11.1876: Registered at Liverpool
(159/1876) in the ownership of British
Shipowners' Co. Ltd., Liverpool as
BRITISH ENTERPRISE.
17.4.1883: Sunk in the River Tyne.
11.5.1883: Register closed, but vessel
subsequently raised, repaired and sold by
the underwriters to W.B. Sproule and Co.,
Liverpool.
29.1.1884: Re-registered at Liverpool
(13/1884) as ANNESLEY.
23.10.1894: Transferred to Liver Shipping
Co. Ltd. (W.B. Sproule and Co., managers),
Liverpool.
30.4.1897: Sold to C.S. Smith, Cardiff.
11.6.1897: Sold for £8,450 to the Ship
Annesley Co. Ltd. (C.S. Smith, manager),
Cardiff.
8.10.1900: Sold to Walter Savill, London.
19.12.1910: Wrecked on the South Rock,
Tuskar, County Wexford in position 52.12
north by 06.13 west while on a voyage from
Melbourne to Queenstown and Belfast with
a cargo of wheat.
4.1.1911: Register closed.

29. BRITISH YEOMAN 1880-1896
O.N. 81391 1,953g 1,898n
269.2 x 40.1 x 23.9 feet
8.1880: Launched by Oswald, Mordaunt and
Co., Southampton (Yard No.180).
11.9.1880: Registered at Liverpool
(97/1880) in the ownership of British
Shipowners' Co. Ltd., Liverpool as
BRITISH YEOMAN.
17.11.1896: Sold to James Taylor, Liverpool.
18.1.1897: Acquired for £7,750 by the
British Yeoman Ship Co. Ltd. (James Taylor,
manager), Liverpool.
18.4.1898: Register closed on sale to S.
Razeto fu M, Genoa, Italy and renamed
STEFANO RAZETO; subsequently reduced
to a barque.
10.1907: Sold to W.S. Watershaw,
Invercargill, New Zealand.
17.10.1907: Restored to the British registry
at Invercargill (1/1907) as BRITISH
YEOMAN.
11.12.1907: Re-registered at Sydney, New
South Wales (45/1907).
10.1908: Seized for unpaid debt by US
authorities at San Francisco.
11.1.1909: Register closed, but vessel
subsequently re-sold to Canadian owners.
24.8.1909: Restored to the British registry at
Victoria, British Columbia (23/1909) in the
name of the Ship British Yeoman Co. Ltd.
(Eschen and Minor, managers), Victoria.
2.3.1916: Sold to J.J. Moore and Co.,
San Francisco, USA but British registry
maintained.
26.2.1917: Captured and sunk by the
German sail auxiliary cruiser SEEADLER
in the Atlantic 230 miles north west by north
from St Paul Rocks in approximate position
4 north by 32 west while on a voyage from
Buenos Aires to Nantes with a cargo of
wheat.
14.4.1917: Register closed.

30. BRITISH MERCHANT 1880-1895
O.N. 81399 1,743g 1,696n
262.9 x 38.3 x 23.3 feet
25.8.1880: Launched by Harland and Wolff,
Belfast (Yard No.137).
6.10.1880: Registered at Liverpool (107/1880)
in the ownership of British Shipowners' Co.
Ltd., Liverpool as BRITISH MERCHANT.
8.8.1895: Register closed on sale to D. Cordes
and Co., Bremen, Germany and renamed
ARTHUR FITGER.
8.1908: Sold to William Griffiths, Newport,
reduced to a barge and renamed QUATSINO.
25.8.1908: Restored to the British registry at
Newport, Monmouthshire (4/1908).
15.10.1909: Stranded and abandoned on the
coast of Alaska.
10.11.1909: Register closed.

37. BRITISH ISLES 1884-1899
O.N. 87992 2,461g 2,394n
308.9 x 43.9 x 24.8 feet
11.6.1884: Launched by John Reid and
Co., Port Glasgow (Yard No.7n).
17.7.1884: Registered at Liverpool
(99/1884) in the ownership of British
Shipowners' Co. Ltd., Liverpool as
BRITISH ISLES.
18.4.1899: Sold to the Ship Four Winds
Co. Ltd (T. Shute and Co., managers),
Liverpool.
13.7.1914: Sold to H.G. Hill and Co. Ltd.,
Cardiff.
16.10.1914: Register closed on sale to
Navigazione Generale Italiane, Genoa,
Italy for use as a coal hulk in South
America.

At the time of her launch, the *Brhhitish Isles* was the largest square rigger ever built on the Clyde. The only steel vessel in the British Shipowners' fleet, she incorporated all the latest improvements in construction and outfit, including the most unusual division of the hold into three compartments. The photograph (above) of her at Melbourne shows a clipper legacy in her fine bow and spars, while that opposite, showing her running free, offers a profile more akin to the big carriers of the 1890s. *[John Naylon collection]*

PUTTING THE RECORD STRAIGHT

Letters, additions, amendments and photographs relating to features in any issues of 'Record' are welcomed. Letters may be lightly edited. Communications by e-mail are quite acceptable, but senders are asked to include their postal address. Please note that correspondence on subjects in multi-part articles is usually held over until the series has been completed.

Flying the Ikurriña

In the caption to Bibby's *Yorkshire* (3) on page 212 of 'Record' 44 you refer to her later owner, Sir Ramon de la Sota, and wonder if he thought of himself as a Basque. He most certainly did as the following little tale might illustrate. Some time in 1970 at Liverpool, I saw the *Artiba* (ex-*Baron Kinnaird*) owned by one of Sir Ramon's flag-of-convenience companies, the Artagan Shipping Co. Ltd. of Monrovia. I was surprised to see her wearing as a stem jack the Ikurriña, the flag of the Basques. When I enquired about this via the ship's agents, I received a letter from Sir Ramon himself, telling me that, by a Basque government decree of 1937, the flag must be flown by all ships controlled, managed or manned by Basques. For many years, especially during the Franco regime, when persecution of the Basques was at its height, the flying or display of the Ikurriña was illegal in Spain, but Sir Ramon insisted that, elsewhere, his captains fly this flag in port. Fortunately, during the 1980s the flag was legalised, and it can now be seen flying over most of the buildings of any consequence in the Basque province. However, I have never since seen it flown by any Basque-controlled ship!
LOUIS LOUGHRAN, 333 Streetsbrook Road, Solihull, B91 1RW

What happened to *Warwickshire*

The Bibby Line article of 'Record 44 noted that no date was known for the fate of the former *Warwickshire* (page 207).

In the aftermath of Typaldos effectively going out of business, most of the fleet were indeed laid up around Perama, but in 1971 she was purchased by Kavounides and named *Sirius*. The latest George Foustanos volume states that she operated as a cruise ship under that name but I have never seen any photographic evidence - indeed all the shots I have seen published show her still languishing in Perama around 1978, clearly showing the new name on the stern but retaining the Typaldos funnel marking. So, my belief is that she never sailed commercially for Kavounides. Some reference books have her scrapped in 1979/80 but the Thames Ship Society certainly saw her on their 1984 trip and she was still in Lloyd's Register as late as 2002.
ROLAND WHAITE, 9 The Paddock, Chepstow, Monmouthshire, NP16 5BW
George Robinson kindly solved this little problem by contacting his friend Aris Bilalis in Greece. Aris has a photo of Sirius *being scrapped at Aspropyrgos in 1981.*
Two photographs of Bibby ships have been wrongly attributed; those of Staffordshire *on page 141 of 'Record' 43 and the middle photograph of* Yorkshire *on 212 of 'Record' 44 were by Paul Boot, to whom apologies. Ed.*

Charlton's pride?

I have a photo of *Charlton Pride* which I got many moons ago from Tom Rayner ('Record' 44, page 218). It is a starboard bow view alongside a wharf with grain conveyor trestles – I should think very likely at Vancouver. She looks much as she did after Donaldson bought her – only one lifeboat more or less in way of her funnel – she has not

A further search of the archives has now yielded the photograph of *Charlton Pride* to which Bill refers. The negative has been marked 'V' which helps confirm that it was taken at Vancouver. *[J. and M. Clarkson collection]*

gotten the topmast stepped to the mainmast yet. Chandris had her hull painted black, but stopped at the level of the deck aft of her superstructure, so there is quite an expanse of white topsides forward. She is looking very much sea-worn in the photo as most of the black hull paint forward of her foremast has washed off leaving her trooper white hull showing. If that was a shipyard paint job, Chandris should have asked for their money back.

BILL SCHELL, 334 South Franklin Street, Holbrook, MA 02343, USA

Death by consultant

The note below the photo of the *Titan* on page 253 of 'Record' 44 put an idea in my head regarding company diversification.

In the late 1960s and early 1970s many of the larger UK companies employed the services of USA-based management consultant companies to advise them, where they were going wrong and what they should do about it in the future. The main US companies engaged were McKinsey and Arthur D. Little. I don't think all the ICI divisions were involved but many shipping companies were. I have noticed only one reference to this in the many books on shipping lines; that in the 'P&O –a Fleet History' by Kevin O'Donoghue and Stephen Rabson, with a reference to McKinsey on page 271. Blue Funnel received 'advice' hence the comments on page 253. The company by whom I was employed suffered from the attention of Arthur D. Little. They were persuaded to build a 1,000 tons per day fertiliser plant in Nova Scotia, which never worked because an adjacent smelter which was to have supplied the sulphuric acid had major problems. The copy of their report which I inherited had written on the cover '30% rubbish 50% common sense and 20% reasonable ideas'. I noted that

by the late 1970s, the two leaders of the team advising us had become university professors.

I am fairly certain that most of the larger shipping companies had visits from one of these consultancies with dramatic effect, e.g. the reorganising of P&O and probably that dreadful funnel, Court Line's diversification and the decision of Blue Funnel to go into tankers and gas carriers. I wonder if we could get people to talk/write to us about this subject so that its effect on the British Merchant Navy is taken into account?

TONY SMITH, 24 Balmoral Road, Kingsdown Kent CT14 8DB

West African traders

I thoroughly enjoyed John Goble's amusing postscript to the article about Nigerian National Shipping Line ('Record' 44). It reminded me of an incident in 1961 when I was Second Mate of the *Florence Holt* and we had finished loading in Tilbury at 15.00. For some reason we did not sail until 22.00. The deck crew secured the ship for sea in record time and those off duty adjourned to the local hostelry. The crew consisted of British deckhands and African engine room crew (recruited from the Shipping Federation), whilst the catering crew were Nigerians recruited in Lagos.

By the time we reached the river it was virtually midnight so I had the watch down to Dungeness with the pilot and the Captain. Fortunately two of the three-man watch were comparatively sober and were able to steer. Approaching Dungeness I instructed the watch to prepare the pilot ladder. This involved dragging it across from one side to the other. They then threw the ladder over the side without making the inboard end fast!

The cadet and I went down on to the deck and, with the two seamen, opened the tonnage hatch aft to get out the second pilot ladder. On opening the hatch we found that the ladder was buried under an assortment of sofas, armchairs and brass bedsteads!

The pilot eventually left the ship by way of the lifeboat boarding ladder.
GEOFF HOLMES, 17 Bayswater Court, Newport Avenue, Wallasey, Cheshire CH45 8QJ

Hemsley extras

Hemsley-1 often made voyages to Heysham from the Mersey to load fuel oil bunkers to take back to the Mersey ('Record' 44 and see also article in 'Marine News' for March 1988, pages 152-154).

On page 44 of the 1984 publication 'Docks and Ports 1 – Southampton' is a photograph taken on 23rd March 1950 and showing two Hemsley Bell tankers bunkering *Queen Mary*. Interestingly, they seem to be transferring the bunkers from Shell's *Glessula* (5,437/1949) across at the other side of the dock. Although built as a Lake Maracaibo tanker, *Glessula* was coasting around UK ports in 1950. Esso's new Fawley refinery was completed in September 1951 and presumably Esso supplied bunkers for the 'Queens' thereafter.
MICHAEL PRYCE, 1 Edington Grove, Churton Park, Wellington 6037, New Zealand

Dave Hocquard points out that the Hemsley Bell tankers did on occasion make trading voyages, and supplied photographs of Attendant *calling at St. Helier. He also sent the accompanying photographs taken on board the* Hemsley-1 *after she had run on to the rocks. They are believed to have come from the late Peter Herbert.*

Bob Todd points out that the builders of Hemsley *were Gebroeders Pot. [Ed]*

Priams go to Blyth

I read with interest the article in 'Record' 44 concerning Holts and the problems of late delivery from Vickers of *Protesilaus* and *Radnorshire*. Are readers aware that the situation was so desperate in the spring of 1967 that Vickers' management sent the unfinished hulls of these vessels to the Blyth shipyard in an attempt to progress the order? The fitting out and craneage facilities of the yard were put back into use after closure, following liquidation and completion of the collier *Rogate* (see 'Record' 31 page 156).

There was in Blyth a core of former shipyard workers available, who obtained employment, as I did, working on these vessels. Following my trade as a plater, I was employed doing heat straightening. The technique I used had been employed for many years in the Blyth yard, but to the management I encountered it seemed a new method. Most of the Vickers workers who came with the ship returned to Tyneside and Blyth men progressed the work. Vickers' management were very impressed with the Blyth workers.

After about six months both ships were returned to the Tyne. The situation was so dire that Vickers hired a bus to transport men free of charge every day from Blyth the 14 miles to the Tyne. The atmosphere in that yard was disheartening from both under-management and men who both seemed to be living on past glories. Whilst I was there a Holt's employee stated they had lost all they had gained at Blyth by returning the ships to the Tyne.
E. CAIN, 25 Bader House, Wensleydale Terrace, Blyth, Northumberland NE 24 3EY

Queen's delay

The photograph on page 230 of 'Record' 44 shows *Glenfinlas* which was launched from John Brown's East Yard on 2nd August 1966. There is also a mention of the delivery delays at the time. Yard number 736 under construction in the East Yard, to be *Queen Elizabeth 2*, is also referred to. She was affected by numerous problems. Her building soon fell behind schedule and she was to be plagued with difficulties before being accepted by Cunard. Many British and even European yards were struggling at the time.

The keel was laid on 5th June 1965 but on 2nd July 1965 a 180-tonne section slewed on the blocks when being put down and had to be repositioned on 5th July. It was announced on 22nd June 1966 that work was behind schedule and delivery was now set for November 1968 rather than May 1968.

After completion and routine pre-trial dry docking in Greenock she began speed trials on 29th November 1968 but had to return to dry dock the following day as oil had contaminated her boiler water supply system which required cleaning and adjustments. As a result a Christmas cruise was cancelled.

Queen Elizabeth 2 left dry dock on 17th December 1968 but on a shake-down cruise she had trouble with her turbines which had to be taken out and rebalanced in John Brown's yard. She was there for three months and it was also reported that 86 cabins required rectification. Cunard announced on 29th December 1968 that they were refusing delivery until the turbine problem was fixed. Her maiden voyage from Southampton to New York began on 2nd May 1969.
MICHAEL DICK, 6 Jacobs Drive, Gourock, Inverclyde PA 19 1LH

Some more on SAMs

Have much enjoyed 'Record' 42, particularly the article on Liberties, they being very much of my era, and having made a voyage in Royal Mail's *Berbice*, ex *Samphill*, launched as *Barrett Wendell*. She was described to me upon joining as 'one of Royal Mail's ocean greyhounds, i.e lean and hungry'! Very apt, as I soon found out.

Your views on the 'A to Z of Liberty Ships' are shared, particularly the 'Uncle Sam' nonsense, which no doubt went down well in the USA. The author's post-war records of US owners are often careless, particularly the intermingling of company/corporation titles, which could refer to unconnected owners.

Fenice (top) and *Orchidea* (middle) of the Pagan Steamship Co. Ltd. had been converted to motor vessels at Nantes in 1961, and given generously-proportioned funnels displaying the colours of parent Zim Israel. *[David Whiteside collection (2)]*

I took the name *Ammla* to be some remote town or region of India, but it is actually an acronym for the American Merchant Marine Library Association, sponsors of said vessel.

One of the first EC2s I saw was the *Edward Bruce* (no middle initial *J* as per your photo caption) in King George V locks, London, and the first ship I saw in Silver Line colours.

The carefully worded reference to Headlam's *Sandsend* and *Sneaton* being the last UK-registered vessels of this type is, of course, absolutely correct, but the Nassau-registered Pagan Steamship Co. Ltd. (a subsidiary of Zim Israel) operated *Fenice*, ex *Andrew Pickens*, from 1965 to 1967 and *Orchidea*, ex *Uriah M. Rose*, from 1964 to 1967 as British vessels.

ALAN PHIPPS, 2 Riverside Road, Droitwich Spa, Worcestershire WR9 8UW

In the list of SAM vessels in 'Record' 44 (page 259) there is a reference to *Saminver* being hit by debris from a V2 rocket on 8th January 1945 which caused two injuries. Robert William Hall, ship's carpenter, did not survive his injuries, dying in Antwerp on 15th January 1945. *Saminver* left Antwerp for the Thames on 28th January. Reference to these events is on the website http://www.twgpp.org/information.php?id=1686512
TONY ATKINSON, 'Tregarth', Lower Redannick, Truro, Cornwall TR1 2JW

Additions and corrections to 'Record' 44

Page 212: the top photograph is believed to be at Santa Cruz de Teneriffe.
Page 217: middle paragraph, 1982 should be 1972.
Page 256: the date of the grounding of *Samsperrin* was 8th July 1944.
Page 257: the date of the fire in *Samvern* was 7th August 1944.
BOB TODD, National Maritime Museum (via e-mail)

Bards on *Bardic*

Some thoughts and memories from a former junior engineer who was on the 'scruffy' Prince, *Bardic*, in 1962 (see 'Record' 44, page 264).

There are easy ships and there are heavy ships. All the people I met during my sea-going career who had served in the 'Sam' boats spoke very highly of them and considered them in the easy category. From an engine room point of view, what could be easier than a good steam reciprocating engine and two oil-fired, watertube boilers?

Whereas the *Bardic* – with a six-cylinder Doxford engine burning heavy oil with steam auxiliaries – was really heavy going. After particularly heavy days (and there were plenty) the engineers would have a few beers and sing a song with the chorus line:
Pack my bags, pack my grip, I'm not coming back next trip
Bye, bye Ba-ar-dic.

Later in my career I served on many ships with Doxford engines all burning heavy oil and none were as heavy as the old *Bardic*. On reflection, I suppose we young engineers must have felt we had achieved something by enabling this ship to be safely navigated around the world.
JOHN DOBSON, 48 Cochrane Park Avenue, Newcastle-upon-Tyne NE7 7JU

As a follow-up to the articles in 'Record' 42, 43 and 44 on Liberty ships, Ian Farquhar has sent us this photograph of the *Samarovsk* arriving at Wellington on the 1st October 1943, and which is referred to on page 255 of 'Record' 44. Considering the amount of cargo on deck it is not surprising some damage had been sustained whilst crossing the Pacific and, noting the catwalks built on top of the cargo, one has to wonder what today's health and safety experts would have to say. *[Ian J. Farquhar]*

SOURCES AND ACKNOWLEDGEMENTS

We thank all who gave permission for their photographs to be used, and for help in finding illustrations we are particularly grateful to Tony Smith, Jim McFaul and David Whiteside of the World Ship Photo Library; to Gerhard Broldiek, Ian Farquhar, Nigel Farrell, F.W. Hawks, Peter Newall, Kevin O'Donoghue, William Schell; and to David Hodge and Bob Todd of the National Maritime Museum, and other institutions listed.

Research sources have included the Registers of William Schell and Tony Starke, 'Lloyd's Register', 'Lloyd's Confidential Index', 'Lloyd's Shipping Index', 'Lloyd's War Losses', 'Mercantile Navy Lists', 'Marine News', 'Sea Breezes' and 'Shipbuilding and Shipping Record'. Use of the facilities of the World Ship Society, the Guildhall Library, the National Archives and Lloyd's Register of Shipping and the help of Dr Malcolm Cooper are gratefully acknowledged. Particular thanks also to Heather Fenton for editorial and indexing work, and to Marion Clarkson for accountancy services.

The other St Ives ship owners

Company information comes from the surviving records of the Registrar of Companies, now in Class BT31 in the National Archives at Kew. Details of Badcock's life are from local newspapers in St. Ives and – a first for 'Record' – 'Baily's Hunting Directory 1916-1917' and 'The Devon and Somerset Staghounds 1907-1936' by E.T. Macdermot. Thanks to Janet Axten of the St. Ives Archive Study Centre and Pat Bawden of Endangered Exmoor for these references.

The history of the two major Cornish tramp ship owners will be found in 'Hain of St. Ives' by K.J. O'Donoghue and H.S. Appleyard (World Ship Society, Kendal, 1986) and in 'Chellew Navigation Co. Ltd.' by Tony Atkinson in 'British Shipping Fleets volume 2' (Ships in Focus, Preston, 2008).

Five of a kind

Thanks to John M. Pryce for Heysham arrival dates.

A turbine trio

Thanks to William Schell for details of the careers of the ships, advice on the text and for images.

THE OTHER ST. IVES SHIP OWNERS
Roy Fenton and David Jenkins

If might sound unlikely that the small Cornish town of St. Ives could produce no fewer than three owners of ocean-going tramp ships. In fact, having spawned one notable owner in Edward Hain, that it produced two others is unsurprising as both William Badcock and Robert Read undoubtedly learned their trade – and formulated their ambitions – in Hain's offices. Of course, neither were large or significant owners compared with Hain – few were – but they are both worth rescuing from almost total obscurity. Indeed, Read only appeared on the radar when the photograph of *Porthia* reproduced on page 29 turned up and her ownership was investigated. Badcock is slightly better known, and is interesting for his accurate predictions of how the freight market would develop and how he raised the capital for his six-ship fleet.

Employee to ship owner

William Badcock (1864-1921) was born in St. Ives. He first intended becoming a nonconformist minister, but decided instead to become a reporter for the 'Western Daily Mercury'. At some point he went to work as a shipping clerk for Edward Hain in his home town, and by 1900 could describe himself as a 'steamship manager'. Badcock's experience with the highly successful Hain company laid the foundation for his own not insubstantial accomplishments in the risky world of tramp shipping. Working for Hain obviously left an impression on Badcock: he lived in a house called 'Tregenna', a name used in the Hain fleet, his first ship had a white line on its hull as did Hain's fleet and its funnel appears black with a white letter 'B' in place of Hain's 'H'.

In 1899 the 35-year-old Badcock decided to enter ship owning himself, and ordered a steamer from the North Dock yard of John Blumer and Co., Sunderland. In March 1900, with his steamer far from complete, he floated the Polurrian Steamship Co. Ltd. with a capital of £24,000 in £25 shares. His six fellow subscribers were in the shipping business in London, and included several ship brokers and ship owners. Despite this being Badcock's first venture, all 960 shares were taken up by July 1900, testimony to his reputation and his choice of fellow subscribers. Badcock showed his faith in the venture by taking 280 shares himself. About half of his 130 or so fellow investors came from Cornwall. The £24,000 raised was insufficient to pay Blumer, and a further £12,000 was raised by a mortgage on the steamer, which was delivered as *Polurrian* in September 1900.

Polurrian sailed from Cardiff on 14th September 1900 bound for St. Vincent, where she would discharge her coal cargo at the bunkering station before proceeding to Mobile, Alabama, probably to load a cotton cargo. This voyage was, in fact somewhat atypical, as *Polurrian* was mostly engaged in taking coal to the Mediterranean from Barry, Cardiff, Newport, Penarth, Port Talbot or Swansea. After discharging at an Italian port such as Genoa, Livorno, Savona or Naples, or perhaps at Alexandria, she would sail through the Dardanelles to the Black Sea or Sea of Azof. At ports such as Constanta, Odessa, Nikolayev, Poti, Sulina or Taganrog she would load grain for the UK, Rotterdam or Antwerp.

Polurrian was obviously a success, as Badcock returned to Blumer for an identical steamer, completed as

William Badcock's first ship, *Polurrian*. Note the white line on her hull in imitation of Hain's livery. The postcard is French and the purchaser – stood on the forecastle – has put a cross above his head. *[K. O'Donoghue collection]*

A portrait of *Polvarth*. The houseflag flying from her mainmast has a white B on a red panel with a white border. The 1912 edition of 'Lloyd's Book of Flags and Funnels' shows the flag without a white border. *[Gerald Broldiek collection]*

Poldhu in January 1902. By the time of her delivery, the money was in place to pay the builders, as another single-ship company, the Poldhu Steamship Co. Ltd., had been registered in June 1901. Shares were priced higher, at £50 each, but nevertheless much of the capital of £28,000 was subscribed within days, again to investors predominantly in Cornwall. The rest of the purchase price was made up by a mortgage from a member of the Holman family and a loan from the Cornish Bank. Debentures were later issued to cover these loans, giving a capital of £35,000, not quite covering the Blumer's bill of £36,000. Badcock awarded himself £300 per annum as managing director.

In a prospectus issued by Badcock, the £36,000 is 'considered very favourable' as prices of ships are 'expected to advance because of the naval programme beginning'. In the typical style of such prospectuses, Badcock writes of the 'great demand in various trades for boats (sic) of the *Polurrian* type'. They are comparatively small but 'can claim the enormous advantage of large carrying capacity on an exceptionally shallow draft, combined with excellent sea speed and moderate coal consumption'. This, he continued, made them suitable for trading to shallow ports where larger ships had to lie off and have their cargo lightered ashore. He was no doubt thinking of the ports of Braila and Galatz on the Danube which exported Black Sea grain. *Poldhu* followed *Polurrian* into the Mediterranean coal/Black Sea grain trade. Just occasionally this would be varied and in April 1902 she loaded at Barry for Mexico, calling at Tampico and Coatacoalcos. She then proceeded via Tampa in Florida to New Orleans to load for Rotterdam, probably taking a cotton cargo.

During a typical voyage in October 1912 *Polurrian* ran into trouble. She loaded coal at Cardiff for Constantinople, and was anticipating a homeward charter with grain at the very high rate then prevailing of 23 shillings per ton, which would have made a record profit for the voyage. But, soon after she had passed Gibraltar, war broke out between Greece and Turkey. At Lesbos *Polurrian*

was stopped and arrested by a Greek destroyer, her coal cargo unloaded for use by the Greek Navy. After six weeks of detention she was taken to Piraeus, and detained further, not being permitted to return home until January 1913. A Greek court subsequently ruled that her detention was illegal, leaving Badcock to fight both the Greek government and his insurers for a substantial loss of profit during her detention.

Taking her story forward, *Polurrian* and her crew were again unlucky in August 1914, finding themselves in Petrograd on the outbreak of war. Badcock seems to have failed in efforts to claim from his P&I Club, but was consoled by receiving £7,669 in fees from the Admiralty, the *Polurrian* having been hired to the Russian government. It is intriguing to note that *Polurrian* was sold in November 1917, presumably whilst still in the Baltic.

St. Ives to South Wales
With trading conditions deteriorating during the 1900s, Badcock was obviously reluctant to expand his two-ship fleet. The surviving annual reports of his first two companies show how depressed was trade, with voyage profits for the *Polurrian* a mere £1,008 in 1908, which represented an overall loss when other expenses were taken into account. *Poldhu* earned a profit of just £760 in 1908, and at one point had to come home in ballast after delivering coal to Ancona and Leghorn, and then spent 10 weeks laid up at Cardiff.

But Badcock decided that the market could only improve, and in 1908 ordered a steamer from the Sunderland Shipbuilding Co. Ltd. About this time he also decided to desert St. Ives for Cardiff, although he is later recorded as living at Minehead and elsewhere in the west of England. The removal of his office to South Wales would put him close to where ships were being fixed, and it is notable that his fellow Cornwall-based ship owners, Hain and Chellew, both maintained a significant presence in Cardiff. In addition, working in the heart of a vibrant shipping and business community Badcock would make invaluable contacts for when he made future speculations.

The new steamer from Sunderland, to be named *Polvarth*, was again financed through a single-ship company, the Polvarth Steamship Co. Ltd., floated several months before the ship herself took to the water. Its capital was £20,000 in £10 shares, with debentures issued to cover the balance of the ship's price of £31,000 (again 'a very low cost' according to Badcock). Following Badcock's move to Cardiff, investors in South Wales began to figure prominently amongst subscribers to his ventures. However, Badcock's faith in the revival of freight rates was obviously not shared by many potential investors and, by the time *Polurrian* was completed in August, only 741 of the 2,000 shares had been taken up. Those who did invest – including a number of Cornishmen and London businessmen – were to be very well rewarded. In the autumn of 1910 freight rates began to show the improvement Badcock had predicted, and all his ships made substantial returns. *Polvarth* began trading in August 1908 and by January 1911 had made an aggregate profit of £4,500. In 1912 alone, voyage profits were a remarkable £9,657. *Polvarth* was torpedoed in December 1917, by when a massive £30,000 had been salted away in the owning company's profit and loss account, a figure not including reserves held back to pay income tax and excess profits tax. The Polvarth Steamship Co. Ltd. was wound up in November 1918, no doubt to the satisfaction of Badcock and his fellow investors.

New to old

Polvarth was the last ship delivered new to Badcock, although according to 'The Shipping World' he ordered others which were sold before completion, profiting from a rising market for ships. Instead, Badcock expanded his fleet with second-hand purchases in 1910, 1911 and 1912. These ships - *Polmanter*, *Polcarne* and *Polperro* - were, respectively, nine, twelve and seventeen years old, their increasing age a reflection of the escalation in tonnage values as shipping came out of recession. Indeed, Badcock foresaw a 'vast expansion in international trade', and predicted that this would prove very profitable for shipping. However, there was probably an element of speculation in the purchases, as the last two acquired, renamed *Polcarne* and *Polperro*, were to be sold in mid-1913.

To finance the purchases of the three ships, two new companies were floated, the Polmanter Steamship Co. Ltd. to own *Polmanter* and the Polcarne Steamship Co. Ltd. to own *Polcarne* and *Polperro*. Both companies had modest

capitalisation of £10,000, in £1 shares for the former and in £10 shares for the latter. Purchase prices were substantially higher than this, for instance £21,000 for the *Leasowe Castle* which became *Polmanter*, and the balance was covered by a mortgage. Resulting from Badcock's closer involvement with the Cardiff business community following his relocation, most of the major investors were businessmen in South Wales including coal owners and exporters, ship owners and ship repairers. The prospectus for the Polmanter company emphasised that it was controlled by a board comprised of representative shareholders, which 'should guarantee that the ship will be worked on lines conducive to the welfare of the shipowners'.

The fleet of six ships which Badcock operated in 1912 and 1913 continued to trade mainly to the Mediterranean and Black Sea. The prospectus for the Polmanter Steamship Co. Ltd. talks of the grain trade to South America as well as that from the Black Sea, but no such voyages have been identified. However, occasional voyages were made into the Baltic. For instance in July and August 1911 *Polvarth* made a return trip from Rotterdam to St. Petersburg, and *Polmanter* loaded in Eupatoria for Riga.

Badcock to Badco

Besides his ship owning, Badcock also operated as a shipping broker and agent. According to the companies' prospectuses, his South Wales Shipping Company, operating from the same address as his ship owning businesses at 41 and 42 The Exchange, Cardiff, was to be responsible for brokerage and agency work whenever the ships were in Bristol Channel ports. Around 1916 Badcock changed his name to Badco, possibly reflecting the way his fellow Cornishmen would have pronounced 'Badcock'.

As well as the two ships sold in 1913, Badco continued to dispose of his ships as the tonnage market rose to unprecedented heights as a result of the First World War. *Polmanter* went in January 1916, quickly joining the fleet of the Bay Steamship Co. Ltd., London. This was a front for the French government who were concerned to build up a fleet for their own wartime shipping requirements and needed to circumvent legislation which forbad British owners to sell ships during hostilities to foreigners, no matter how close they were as allies. Badco's earliest ships, *Polurrian* and *Poldhu*, went in November 1917 to companies managed by the Swansea-based Letricheux and David. Within a month the loss of *Polvarth* to a torpedo rendered Badco shipless but undoubtedly wealthy. As an example of the returns possible during the war, *Poldhu* had

Seen in this less than satisfactory print, possibly in Rotterdam, *Poldhu* was a sister of *Polurrian*. Her paint scheme differs from that of *Polurrian*, with no white line on her hull and her funnel having the white letter B on a red band, the colours noted for Badcock in the 1912 edition of 'Lloyd's Book of Flags and Funnels'.
[J.T. Peake/Roy Fenton collection]

made a profit of £9,370 on charter to the Admiralty in 1915 and £9,150 in 1916. The sale prices of the steamers and the insured value of Polvarth have not been discovered (the companies' surviving accounts are silent on these matters), but they too would be greatly inflated, so that Badco and his fellow investors would have been well rewarded when each of the owning companies was wound up after their ships were sold.

William Badco did not return to ship owning after 1917, and indeed may not have been a well man. After a long illness he died at his home in Chippenham, Wiltshire on 9th March 1921 at the relatively early age of 57. He had several interests outside shipping, being a nonconformist preacher, sitting on St. Ives Town Council in 1901 and in that year standing unsuccessfully as a Liberal candidate for Cornwall County Council. He also developed a keen interest in hunting, and from 1916 to 1918 acted as Master of the Devon and Somerset Staghounds. As a ship owner, in his more modest way, Badco emulated his illustrious predecessor from St. Ives and former employer, Edward Hain.

Fleet list

1. POLURRIAN   1900-1917
O.N. 104679 2,801g 1,807n
319.7 x 46.1 x 21.0 feet
T. 3-cyl. by John Dickinson and Sons Ltd., Sunderland; 220 NHP, 1,100 IHP, 9 knots.
8.1900: Completed by John Blumer and Co., North Dock, Sunderland (Yard No.156).
1.9.1900: Registered in the ownership of the Polurrian Steamship Co. Ltd. (William Badcock, manager), St. Ives as POLURRIAN.
25.11.1917: Sold to the English Steamship Co. Ltd. (Letricheux and David Ltd., managers), Swansea.
22.12.1917: Renamed SKEGNESS.
22.10.1919: Sold to W. Reardon Smith and Sons Ltd., Cardiff.
15.1.1920: Transferred to the Cornborough Shipping Line Ltd. (Sir W. Reardon Smith and Sons (London) Ltd., managers), Cardiff.
30.1.1924: Register closed on sale to Inukami Keigoro, Tokyo, Japan and renamed SAPPORO MARU No. 11.
5.7.1945: Torpedoed and sunk by the United States submarine BARB in the La Pérouse Strait in position 46.04 north by 142.14 east.

Pollurrian with a plain black hull. *[Nigel Farrell collection]*

Polvarth. [Nigel Farrell collection]

2. POLDHU   1902-1918
O.N. 104680 2,793g 1,791n
319.7 x 46.1 x 21.0 feet
T. 3-cyl. by John Dickinson and Sons Ltd., Sunderland; 263 NHP, 1,060 IHP, 9 knots.
1.1902: Completed by John Blumer and Co., Sunderland (Yard No. 164).
21.1.1902: Registered in the ownership of John James, Truro as POLDHU.
12.6.1902: Transferred to the Poldhu Steamship Co. Ltd. (William Badcock, manager), St. Ives.
26.11.1917: Sold to Letricheux Line Ltd. (Letricheux and David, managers), Swansea.
22.1.1918: Renamed STROMNESS.
20.12.1919: Sold to W. Reardon Smith and Sons Ltd., Cardiff.
23.12.1919: Register closed on sale to A/S Vore (Lundegaard and Stray, managers), Farsund, Norway and renamed BRAVORE.
1923: Sold to Kawasaki Kisen K.K., Kobe, Japan and renamed SAKAYE MARU
1938: Name rendered SAKAE MARU.
23.11.1944: Torpedoed and sunk by US Submarine BANG south east of Yonaguni Island, east of Taiwan, in position 24.12 north by 122.53 east.

3. POLVARTH   1909-1917
O.N. 128904 3,146g 1,972n
330.0 x 48.7 x 22.2 feet
T. 3-cyl. by the North Eastern Marine Engineering Co. Ltd., Sunderland; 287 NHP, 1,600 IHP, 9.75 knots.
8.1909: Completed by the Sunderland Shipbuilding Co. Ltd., Sunderland (Yard No. 251).
9.8.1909: Registered in the ownership of the Polvarth Steamship Co. Ltd. (William Badcock, manager), Cardiff as POLVARTH.
20.12.1917: Torpedoed and sunk by the German submarine U 86 35 miles west of Ouessant whilst on a voyage from Gibraltar to Swansea with a cargo of zinc ore, phosphates and naval stores.
2.2.1918: Register closed.

4. POLMANTER 1910-1916
O.N. 114712 3,515g 2,262n
340.5 x 47.2 x 24.8 feet
T. 3-cyl by George Clark Ltd., Sunderland; 320 NHP, 1,600 IHP, 9 knots.
7.1901: Completed by Short Brothers Ltd., Sunderland (Yard No. 299).
1901: Registered in the ownership of The Steam Ship New Orleans Co. Ltd. (David G. Pinkney and Co., managers), London as NEW ORLEANS.
18.5.1908: Stranded at Pulo Laut whilst on a voyage from Ocean Island to Hamburg with a cargo of phosphate. Refloated and towed to Stagen. Declared a constructive total loss.
31.12.1909: Sold to George Walker, Liverpool.

27.5.1910: Sold to H. and C. Grayson Ltd., London
10.8.1910: Renamed LEASOWE CASTLE.
28.12.1910: Acquired by the Polmanter Steamship Co. Ltd. (William Badcock, manager), Cardiff for about £21,000.
28.1.1911: Renamed POLMANTER.
20.1.1916: Sold to Furness, Withy and Co. Ltd., London
29.1.1916: Sold to the Bay Steamship Co. Ltd., London.
12.6.1916: Renamed BAYMANTER.
11.11.1920: Wrecked on Ras Hafrun, Aden whilst on a voyage from Ankify, Nossi-Bé to Liverpool with a cargo of manioc flour.
18.2.1921: Register closed.

5. POLCARNE   1911-1913
O.N. 104226 3,036g 1,949n
324.3 x 47.0 x 22.4 feet
T. 3-cyl. by Blair and Co. Ltd., Stockton-on-Tees; 230 NHP, 1,150 IHP, 9 knots.
12.1899: Completed by the Blyth Shipbuilding Co. Ltd., Blyth (Yard No. 96).
30.11.1899: Registered in the ownership of the East Yorkshire Steamship Co. Ltd. (Herbert D. Meek of Alexander Meek, and Sons, managers), Goole as EVERINGHAM.
1.6.1911: Sold to the Polcarne Steamship Co. Ltd. (William Badcock, manager), Cardiff.

10.6.1911: Renamed POLCARNE.
26.7.1913: Register closed on sale to A/S Skoglands Linje (T.H. Skogland and Søn A/S, managers), Haugesund, Norway and renamed SKOGLAND.
1925: Transferred to A/S Skoglands Rederi (T.H. Skogland and Søn A/S, managers), Haugesund.
1931: Sold to D/S A/S Skudefjord (Fr. Waage Rasmussen, manager), Haugesund and renamed SKUDEFJORD.
1934: Sold to D/S A/S Ledaal (Brødr. Olsen, manager), Stavanger, Norway and renamed LEDAAL.
1935: Managers became A. Gowart Olsen and E. Gundersen.
1946: Sold to Compania Atalaya de Navigation General S.A., Panama (Emm. Yannoulatos) and renamed GERODIMOS.
1949: Sold to Sevket Manioglu ve Ortaklari, Istanbul, Turkey and renamed ABANT.
1953: Sold to Abant Vapur Isletmesi (Mehmet Kazanci, manager), Istanbul.
1954: Transferred to Turk Silepcilik Limitet Sirketi (Mehmet Kazanci, manager), Istanbul.
1956: Sold to Mehmet Kazanci ve Serikleri, Istanbul.
1959: Broken up at Istanbul by her owners during the fourth quarter.

6. POLPERRO   1912-1913
O.N. 104273   3,038g   1,961n
315.0 x 40.5 x 20.2 feet
T. 3-cyl by Blair and Co. Ltd., Stockton-on-Tees; 200 NHP, 1,000 IHP, 9 knots.
2.1895: Completed by Ropner and Son, Stockton-on-Tees (Yard No. 300).
7.2.1895: Registered in the ownership of Thomas Dixon junior, trading as Dixon, Robson and Company, Newcastle-on-Tyne as ISLE OF KENT
27.4.1897 to 27.8.1897: 31/64 transferred to the Isle of Kent Steamship Co. Ltd. (Dixon, Robson and Company, managers), Newcastle-upon-Tyne.
23.7.1903: Transferred to the Isles Steam Shipping Co. Ltd. (Dixon, Robson and Company, managers), Newcastle-upon-Tyne.
17.5.1912: Acquired by the Polcarne Steamship Co. Ltd. (William Badcock, manager), Cardiff.
22.5.1912: Renamed POLPERRO.
28.11.1913: Register closed on sale to Mori Heizo, Amagasaki, Japan and renamed HEIYO MARU.
11.8.1916: Sailed from Miike for Singapore with a cargo of coal and disappeared.

Badcock's oldest ship, the 1895-built *Polperro,* in Penarth Dock during 1912 or 1913. *[Nigel Farrell collection]*

Germany to Cornwall

The third St. Ives ship owner was undoubtedly the least successful. On 20th May 1921, the Porthia Steamship Co. Ltd. was registered, initial subscribers being Robert Hodgson Read (who describes himself initially as a marine engineer and later as an underwriter) and Samuel H. Stevens, a secretary, both of St. Ives. In the remarkably short space of eight days the company's entire share capital of £65,000 in £100 shares had been subscribed. It was a time of high freight rates and even higher expectations amongst potential ship owners, and this venture seems to have caught the fancy of many Cornish investors. The largest shareholder by far was Robert Sawle Read, presumably Robert H. Read's father, with 343 shares, and who had bought the ex-German steamer *Polaria* from the Shipping Controller and renamed her *Porthia.* Other shareholders, with no more than 20 shares each, included members of the Hain, Chellew, Bolitho, Bennetts and Harvey families, all of whom had strong connections with shipping or finance in Cornwall.

The exact relationship of the Read and Hain families is unclear, but was probably close. Robert Sawle Read accompanied Lord Inchcape when, in October 1917, the latter visited St. Ives to make an offer on behalf of P&O to purchase the Hain fleet following the death of Edward Hain. Another clue comes from the title of Hain's agents at Cardiff: Foster, Hain and Read. Significantly, amongst the few non-Cornish investors, were members of the Readhead family, who had built all the ships of Edward Hain, through whom they would have known the Reads.

Porthia was virtually new, and seems to have traded consistently over the next six years without being laid up, escaping the fate of so many ships in the mid-1920s. In contrast to the Badcock ships, her employment was largely in the UK/Continent to River Plate trade, calling on her way at the Cape or, on her maiden voyage, at Mauritius. She is also recorded as visiting the West Indies, USA and trading 'East', probably to India. The surviving records of the

Porthia Steamship Co. Ltd. are dry, even by the standards of the official returns routinely demanded by the Registrar of Companies. However, it can be assumed the company did not prosper, having bought *Porthia* at the top of the market just before freight rates and ship prices fell drastically. The most significant entry comes in September 1927 when a meeting of shareholders resolves on voluntary liquidation, and appoints Samuel H. Stevens to wind up the company, a process completed by April 1928. A few weeks previously Robert Hodgson Read has been replaced as a director by John Hodgson Read, probably his son, whilst in July sale of the *Porthia* back to Germany had been finalised. She had been built as a cargo liner, part of a class of seven completed at Flensburg for Hamburg-Amerika, and returned to this role for the Woermann Linie. Escaping the fate of most German-owned ships during the Second World War through taking refuge in neutral Lobito, she was taken over by Portugal and survived under their flag until 1950.

The German-built *Porthia*. She had six sisters, of which two were sold by the Shipping Controller to R.P. Houston to become *Hesperides* and *Hesperia*. [J. and M. Clarkson]

PORTHIA   1921-1927
O.N. 144618   3,919g   2,403n
384.8 x 52.8 x 22.1 feet.
T. 3-cyl. by Flensburger Schiffsbau Gesellschaft, Flensburg, Germany; 527 NHP, 2,600 IHP, 11½ knots.
12.7.1919: Launched by Flensburger Schiffsbau Gesellschaft, Flensburg, Germany (Yard No. 352).
She had been laid down for Hamburg-Amerika Linie, Hamburg, Germany.
3.1920: Ran trials.
12.7.1920: Completed.

21.7.1920: Registered in the ownership of Deutsche Reich, Berlin, Germany as POLARIA.
24.7.1920: Delivered to the United Kingdom Leith.
9.8.1920: Registered in the ownership of the Shipping Controller (Royal Mail Steam Packet Company, managers), London as POLARIA.
10.2.1921: Acquired by Robert S. Read, St. Ives.
28.4.1921: Renamed PORTHIA.
30.6.1921: Transferred to the Porthia Steam

Ship Co. Ltd. (Robert H. Read and Co. Ltd., managers), St. Ives.
14.7.1927: Register closed on sale to Woermann-Linie A.G., Hamburg and renamed WAMERU.
9.1939: Laid up at Lobito, Angola.
27.4.1942: Transferred to John T. Essberger, Hamburg.
16.5.1943: Taken over by Companhia Colonial de Navegação, Lisbon, Portugal and renamed HUAMBO.
6.1950: Broken up at Savona by A.R.D.E.M. S.p.A.

Tre, Pol and Pen
'By their Tre-, Pol- and Pen- shall you know your Cornishmen' runs the rhyme, and the Cornish tramp ship owners used all three of these place name elements in naming their ships. Hain adopted 'Tre', meaning

simply 'place' and had no trouble in finding over 50 names with this prefix. Richard Chellew, who was also a native of St. Ives but began his shipping business in Truro, used 'Pen' meaning 'headland', and employed 19 of these names for his fleet. Badcock completed the trio with his six 'Pols', an element which means 'pool'. He was not the only Cornishman to use Pol, however, and Hannan, Samuel and Co. Ltd. later imitated Badcock in naming their motor coasters *Poldhu* and *Polurrian*. At first sight, the largest ship ever to have 'Penzance' on her stern seemed to follow this theme. The 4,751 gross ton *Polzella*, completed by William Gray and Co. Ltd., West Hartlepool in 1929 was registered in the port

to honour the county in which her Cardiff owner John James Thomas was born. But the name did not have the romantic Cornish connection one might expect; *Polzella* was simply a compound of Thomas's daughters' names, Polly and Grizella. Owned in the name of the Eclipse Shipping and Trading Co. Ltd. of Cardiff, the *Polzella* was torpedoed off the Shetlands on 17th January 1940 with the loss of all hands.

The Penzance-registered, Cardiff-owned *Polzella*, with topmasts struck to transit the Manchester Ship Canal and with a black hull (above). *[J. and M. Clarkson collection]*
Polzella is seen again, at Avonmouth, with a grey hull (below). John J. Thomas used a yellow funnel with black top and his houseflag was yellow with his initials JJT in black. *[Roy Fenton collection]*

A TURBINE TRIO

It is comforting to know that it was not only the British who made expensive mistakes in setting up shipyards at the end of the First World War to meet an exceptional demand for ships which quickly evaporated. The Italians did likewise, or so it seems on investigating the accompanying photographs of the turbine steamer *Valsesia* (6,606/1922) firmly ashore in South Wales.

The ship had been completed by Società Anonima Ilva at Piombino, Italy as yard number 2 with the name *Piombino II*. Not surprisingly, there was also a *Piombino I* which was completed in December 1921 as yard number 1. The yard at Piombino, which is in Tuscany almost opposite the Isle of Elba, does not appear in the List of Shipbuilders in 'Lloyd's Register' during the 1920s, suggesting that it built just the two ships and then closed down. S.A. Ilva was a major Italian steel producer and was also heavily involved with shipping: its subsidiary Lloyd Mediterraneo of Genoa took delivery of *Piombino I* and *Piombino II*. Under the title Cantiere Navali Ilva, the steel producer also had a yard at Naples which completed a similar ship, *Bagnoli 1* (6,284/1922). All three had geared turbines made by Tosi of Legnano

Piombino II was renamed *Valsesia* in 1923 by Lloyd Mediterraneo, and her

Valsesia, ex *Piombino II*, stranded at Treharne Point, Barry in August 1926. *[Roy Fenton collection]*

Villarperosa. Note the goalpost masts and lattice-type derricks. *[Ships in Focus]*

sister became *Valsugana* in 1924. In 1925 both were sold without change of name to companies controlled by Tito Campanella, also of Genoa.

Valsesia stranded at Treharne Point, Barry on 25th August 1926, later broke in two and was sold for scrap. Her cargo was coal from Hampton Roads, but what was unexpected is that it was bound for Barry – one of the world's largest coal *exporting* ports. This was of course during the miners' strike which precipitated (and extended long after) the General Strike in the United Kingdom in 1926.

Valsugana also had an eventful career. In 1927 her steam turbines were replaced with diesels and she was renamed *Villarperosa*, remaining with Tito Campanella. She was at Wilmington, North Carolina in June 1940 when Italy entered the Second World War, remaining there to be taken over by the US Government in March 1941, well before the two countries were officially enemies. Renamed *Colin*, she was put back into service in 1942, but under the Panama flag, presumably because this allowed her to operate in waters from which US-flag ships were barred because of the Neutrality Act. It also permitted the employment of the considerable numbers of neutral, Scandinavian, and other Allied seamen who were stranded in the USA, having had their ships sunk but being unable to reach their homes.

Colin was a comparatively late victim of the U-boat war, torpedoed and sunk in mid-Atlantic by *U 859* on 26th April 1944 whilst on a voyage from New Orleans via Halifax to Garston with a cargo of sulphur and military vehicles. *U 859* has been described as a 'U-cruiser'; officially she was a Type IXD2 of which 30 were built, submarines with extended range designed to be sent out to the Far East. *U 859* was actually on passage from Kiel to Penang when she encountered the unfortunate *Colin*, a straggler from convoy SC 157. Revenge came five months later. HM Submarine *Trenchant* was waiting off Penang and sank *U 859* as she entered the port under Japanese escort.

Bagnoli I had the longest career of the three, but this was certainly not without incident. Original owners were the steel company itself, S.A. Ilva, but in common with her near sisters she was transferred in 1923 to Lloyd Mediterraneo and renamed

The motor ship *Colin*, ex-*Piombino 1* and *Villarperosa*, now US-owned and under the Panama flag, on 26th March 1943. *[US Coastguard/William Schell]*

The former *Bagnoli I* and *Valtellina* as the motor ship *Chisone* at Philadelphia on 18th June 1934. *[Francis Palmer/William Schell]*

The Chisone became *Italvalle* when salvaged after the Second World War, and was photographed as such at Genoa on 28th March 1951. *[Raul Maya/William Schell]*

Valtellina. After her sale in 1925 new owners Societa Commerciale di Navigazione (Giuseppe de Benedetti), Genoa retained this name until 1928 when she too was converted to a motor ship and became *Chisone*. The Second World War saw her become a casualty twice. On 22nd January 1943 she was

bombed by the Allies 30 miles off Cap Bon but was towed into Bizerta and repaired. In German service after being seized at Genoa in September 1943, she was sunk at Toulon during an Allied air raid on 29th April 1944. When raised after the war she became *Italvalle* for Genoese owners in 1948 and *Cesare*

Battisti for a company in Venice in 1952. Breaking up began at Vado in 1962.

The ships' layout, with engines aft, and observing that both *Valsesia* and her sister *Colin* were carrying coal and sulphur, respectively, when lost led the editor to the assumption that they were early examples of bulk carriers. However, William Schell, who helped greatly with this short article, points out that they cannot qualify as they were not single-deck ships. *Bagnali 1* had dual classification with Lloyd's Register and Registro Italiano Navale, and the former's register book lists her as having a main deck, an awning deck and a third deck in number 1 hold. The layout was not unique to Ilva, as yards in the Ansaldo group also turned out a number of similar ships.

Cesare Battisti, the final name of the *Bagnali I,* photographed at Boston. *[John O'Leary/William Schell]*

BEN LINE FOLLOW-UP

A personal note by Graeme Somner

Having completed the fourth edition of Ben Line early in 2009, my thoughts went back to when I first actually came in contact with the company. It was definitely a long time ago.

My first recollection was, as a school boy, visiting *Bennevis* (1), built in 1918, in Leith docks some time in the mid-1930s. It was the first time that I had come across a ship manned by a Chinese crew – I had up till then never come across Chinese in quantity before! I was impressed how silently they moved round the decks in their canvas sandals compared with the noise the European crew made in their heavy boots. The ship was immaculate as she had just come out of the Imperial Dry Dock after her annual overhaul, and her traditionally-grained superstructure was gleaming. Those were the days when the company still loaded and discharged at Leith so there was a steady stream of Ben Line steamers always to be seen in the Imperial Dock.

My next contact with the ships of the Ben Line was to be in rather different circumstances and a long way from Leith. In the course of my time in the Army I found myself attached in June 1943 to Army Post Office 475 located at Gibraltar. One of the functions of this APO was to make up and load surface mail (both from civil and military sources) for the United Kingdom,

West Africa and the Middle East and beyond. The mails were usually loaded on ships moored in the Bay and this took place (for the UK at least) about every five days or so, depending on the departure of the convoys. Until I joined the APO, the civilian Post Office staff had to oversee this activity, but being somewhat elderly were not keen on the task, which involved boarding vessels often by rope ladder in rough conditions in open waters. I volunteered to take over the task and this was gladly accepted by both civil and military authorities.

The arrangement was that the naval authorities advised the Port Operating Company, Royal Engineers when a ship was available to load mail and at what time it had to be loaded. The Port Operating Company allocated a variety of craft to the task, using either one of their tugs, of which they had two, loading the mail on the stern deck if 50 bags or less, towing a lighter if more than that number of bags, or loading the bags on the deck of a chartered civilian steam tender if it was likely that we would have to go deep into Spanish waters – where the division between British and Spanish waters was, was always debatable. When I arrived with the mails at the dock, the Port Operating Company checker would advise me of the serial number of the ship (allocated when the vessel entered the Bay) on which we were to load. He also told me where the vessel should be anchored

– there could be up to 60 vessels anchored in the Bay stretching round from Europa Point at the southern tip of Gibraltar, to the port of Algeciras in Spain on the west side of the Bay. I write 'should be anchored' as often ships were unable to take up their allotted area because other ships were out of position so the ship then dropped anchor where it could – they became 'lost' and, unless one knew the ship's name (which gave a clue to its outline), it meant in looking at each and every ship in the Bay to check its number. If one could get a name, any amount of time could be saved. I could sometimes ask (and got) the ship's name and from my knowledge of ship recognition was then able to eliminate those ships that did not fit the bill. One day I could not get a name and it took four hours to find the ship, the 60th, lying off the entrance to Algeciras. Which brings me to an interesting point – I was in British Army uniform but frequently found myself afloat in Spanish waters, could I have been interned, I wonder? We often waved to the Spanish guards on the beach (we were within 100 yards of them) on the Spanish shore and they acknowledged our greetings. I suppose if I had been picked up, I would have been returned to Gibraltar for the usual £150, the going rate for dropping off escaping RAF crew members who were passed back via the Spanish-flagged Algeciras to Gibraltar ferry, which ran several times daily throughout the war.

I took over responsibility for loading the mail in September 1943 and the second ship I boarded was *Benrinnes* (2) on 24th September. A vessel of 5,451 gross tons built in 1921 for Furness Withy and Co. and acquired by Ben Line in 1938, it had been some 15 months since she last saw Leith. I loaded 101 bags of mail for the UK on her on 24th September but, because of her convoy being delayed, made supplementary calls to her on 29th September and 2nd October with some additional bags. The offer by the naval authorities to permit additional mails to be loaded usually came with the provision of a large picket boat (not the brass funnel sort intended for an admiral but a motor-driven one that could carry 50 to 60 sailors in open conditions) and I

felt very grand sailing round the Bay in my own boat manned by three uniformed naval ratings. Using this type of craft I could at least board in comfort via the ship's accommodation ladder, and not have to scale up a ship's side on a rope ladder of sometimes indifferent condition.

My next contact with a Ben Line ship was on 5th May 1945 when I loaded 31 bags of mail on *Benalder* (4), a vessel of 5,161 gross tons built in 1919 for Elder Dempster of Liverpool and acquired by the Ben Line in 1935. She was waiting to join convoy MKS 99 sailing that afternoon for the UK.

Convoys were discontinued from 28th May 1945 so the opportunities to load mail became less predictable, as most ships sailed through the Straits without making a call at Gibraltar. On 4th August 1945 I undertook my last mail run when I boarded Cunard White Star's *Samaria* (19,957/1921). A few days afterwards the APO was taken over by civilians and I was posted to other duties. In just under two years I had boarded 85 ships ranging from the large troopship *Georgic* (27,268/1932) on four occasions in 1945, eight Empires, two Parks, two Forts and three Liberties, to the smallest of them all, the small Glasgow coaster *Jade* (930/1938) on 29th March 1944 on her way home to take part three months later in the D-Day landings. The ships that I hated most were those with high freeboards, such as the Pacific Steam Navigation Company's *Orbita* (16,532/1915) on 13th November 1943 – the ladder was rigged by number 2 hatch and it was a long climb to the deck!

I was to visit other Ben Line ships in the 1960s and 1970s in the course of writing the third edition of their history. This was in the London Royal Docks and usually included a lunch on board with the master and the various superintendents supervising the loading – all very smart and with Chinese stewards serving the meal. It might, therefore, appear that my contact with Ben Line runs for a span of some 70-odd years: a long period for one never employed directly in shipping or by the company.

Cunard's *Samaria* in the Mersey. [B. and A. Feilden/J. and M. Clarkson collection]

Georgic as rebuilt at Belfast in 1943-1944 (above). She retained White Star's funnel colours until broken up in 1956. *[Graeme Somner collection]*

Photographed on the Manchester Ship Canal, the motor ship *Jade* had been built in the Netherlands in 1938 for William Robertson, Glasgow (right). She features prominently in the new Ships in Focus publication 'William Robertson and the Gem Line'. *[R.J. Scott/Graeme Somner collection]*

Orbita on the Mersey before the Second World War (below). Used as an emigrant ship post-war, she lasted until broken up at Newport in 1950 *[B. and A. Feilden/J. and M. Clarkson]*

Additions and amendments

The publishers thank Bob Todd of the National Maritime Museum, Pieter Fransen, A.D. Frost and Bert Stevens for the following notes.

Page 50, 11 lines from bottom: should be *Pando Point* and not *Pando Cape*.

Page 54, second paragraph: should be *Benvorlich* (4) not *Benvorlich* (5).

Page 95: *Benvenue* was hired as a boom carrier 1935-1936. The photos show her nets being recovered.

Page 96: *Benmohr's* crew was rescued from three lifeboats by a Short Sunderland serial number L5805, coded B, of 95 Squadron.

Page 100: the upper of the two photographs of *Benwyvis* (1) aground shows a separate incident to that described in caption. On 3rd May 1930 *Benwyvis* went ashore off the Boulevard at Vlissingen whilst on a voyage from Antwerp to Middlesbrough. The tugs which refloated her can be seen in the background to the photograph: the harbour tug *Hoek van Holland* and, to her right, the ocean-going *Noordzee*. *Benwyvis* was refloated the following night and resumed her voyage.

Page 104, third column: 5.1940: *Benlawers* rescued wounded men from Calais 24.5.1940 and from Cherbourg 17.6.1940 but did not call at Le Havre.

Page 107, first column: *Bendoran* arrived at Courseulles (Juno Beach), not Arromanches, on 7.6.1944 and was scuttled on 9.6.1944.

Page 145: the replacement engine fitted to *Elys Harbour*, the former *Benarty* (5), had an interesting history. It was an experimental Doxford three-cylinder diesel originally used in trials of turbocharging. In 1955 it was used to replace the original machinery in the tanker *Easthill Escort* (8,477/1946), the former merchant aircraft carrier *Empire MacCabe*, which was scrapped in 1962, when the engine moved on to *Elys Harbour*.

Page 153: the Germans occupied Dodecanese in September 1943.

Page 155: the date below the photograph of *Benloyal* (2) on the slipway should be 3rd October 1958.

Page 157, bottom caption: *Benhiant* became *Beaverlodge* in 1952.

Page 174: the tonnage of *Benalbanach* (3) was 11,446g.

Page 183: the tug attempting to get a line aboard the damaged *Bencruachan* (3) is not the *Clyde*, and may be the *Marjan 1*. The *Clyde* appears in the uppermost photograph on page 184, partly hidden by the stern of *Bencruachan*.

Page 188: the middle photograph shows *Benavon* passing *Benalder*.

Page 197 and 199: the chemical tankers *Benvenue* (5) and *Bencleuch* (7) were launched at Groningen, not Zierikzee.

Page 201, second column: delete the 5.1984 sale to COSCO as *Kang Hai*.

Page 213: the top photograph shows *War Roach* with torpedo damage to number 2 hold.

Page 214: *Fort Qu'Appelle* sailed independently from Vancouver to Halifax and was intended to pick up a convoy for the Halifax to UK part of her voyage.

Page 215: *Fort Babine* was launched 25.3.1942 and completed 26.6.1942.

Page 216: in the bottom left hand photograph the aircraft is Fairey Swordfish V4570 and the date is 7th May 1943.

Page 217: the date of the top photograph is almost certainly between 7th and 10th May 1943.

Page 218: the occupation of Norway commenced on 9th April 1940 and all Allied forces had evacuated by 10th June 1940. If the date shown is correct she must have been landing occupation troops rather than invasion forces.

Acknowledgements and bibliography

Graeme Somner's acknowledgements were inadvertently omitted from 'Ben Line'.

Over the last 50 years I have been recording and researching the shipping activities of Wm. Thomson and Co. I became involved originally when George Blake included my fleet list in his book published in 1955. In 1967 the history was published by the World Ship Society, to be followed in 1980 by a new and revised edition. This current book updates and concludes the company's 155-year history.

I am indebted to W.R.E. Thomson, a partner in Wm. Thomson and Co. from 1963 and Chairman of the Ben Line Group from 1972, and Captain Archie Walters, the last Marine Superintendent, who served on many of the ships during his service, for their advice and for sharing with me their personal knowledge of the company and its activities. I am also grateful to them for reading through the draft text of the history and bringing me back on course when I drifted away from it. Their input was a great asset and ensures that the trading activities of Wm. Thomson and Co. are accurately recorded for posterity.

As regards the compilation of the fleet lists, my task was made easier by the great help given to me by the World Ship Society Central Record Team (both past and present holders of the material), and also Captain John Landels on whom I depended for shipbuilders' yard details and launch dates. I am also indebted to the staffs of Lloyd's Register of Shipping; the National Archives, Kew; the Guildhall Library, City of London; and of the Guildhall Library, Southampton, whose production of the many documents that I requested over the years ensured the accuracy of the lists. There were a host of individuals, too many to mention, who supplied me with snippets of information on specific vessels that otherwise I would be unaware of - to them my grateful thanks.

Many of the illustrations included in this book come from the archives of Wm. Thomson and Co., and others come from my own collection. I am most grateful to John Clarkson for his efforts to locate and obtain many photographs never published before. Where the source of an illustration is known, suitable acknowledgement has been made, and to all these individuals and companies I am sincerely grateful for allowing me to reproduce their material.

Recommended further reading:
'The Ben Line, the Story of a Merchant Fleet at War 1939-1945'; Thomas Nelson and Sons Ltd., Edinburgh, 1951.
'The Ben Line, a History of a Merchant Fleet 1825-1955' by George Blake; Thomas Nelson and Sons Ltd., Edinburgh, 1956.
'The Ben Line 1825-1982, an Anecdotal History' by Michael Strachan; Michael Russell, Norwich, 1992.

Availability

'Ben Line' is published at £28.50 plus £3.50 postage in the UK and £4.50 elsewhere (post-free to 'Record' subscribers) and is available from J. and M. Clarkson, 18 Franklands, Longton, Preston PR4 5PD, UK. A 232-page hard back, it has a profusion of photographs and illustrations in colour and black and white, many of which have never been published before.

In 1982 the 12-year old *Benlawers* (4) underwent a drastic conversion to a livestock carrier, as which she was renamed *Uniceb* (above). Seen here in 1984, she still has her original bridge, just visible above the pens, with a new bridge added above. *[Nick Tolerton]*

At Hobart on 5th May 1963, *Elys Harbour*, the former *Benarty* (5), is still registered in Leith, although owned by a Bermuda-based company controlled by Mollers Ltd. of Hong Kong (right). *[David Kirby/Russell Priest collection]*

Another former Ben Line ship, *De Verrazano*, ex-*Benalbanach* (3) looks very smart in the colours of Italia S.p.A. She was photographed at Vancouver on 3rd August 1973 (below). *[Russell Priest collection]*

FIVE OF A KIND
A series of large coastal tankers
Captain Michael Pryce

These are the stories of five traditional coastal tankers built in British shipyards between 1949 and 1954, all of which had an amidships bridge and trunk decks. (For those who have forgotten, having trunk decks meant that the level of the deck over the wing cargo tanks was much lower than the level of the deck of the centre cargo tanks, by about six feet in these ships). Of what was then conventional appearance, they were somewhat larger than the average coastal tankers of the period. Four of them were built for Shell companies and traded in widely differing parts of the world, whilst the final Irish ship was built for charter to a Shell group company.

FELIPES

John Crown and Sons Ltd., Sunderland (Yard No. 230), 1950; 2,992g, 1,544n, 3,345d; 331.9 (o.a.) x 46.0 x 16.7 feet 6-cylinder 4SCSA oil engine by Hawthorn, Leslie and Co. Ltd., Newcastle-upon-Tyne, 10.75 knots.

Felipes was the first of a pair of motor tankers. She was launched in Sunderland on 21st October 1949 and delivered on 3rd March 1950 at a cost of £283,818 to Nederlandsche-Indies Tankstoomboot Maatschappij and registered at The Hague under the Dutch flag. In appearance *Felipes* and near sister *Tanea* were very similar to the slightly larger *Alberta*, *Antonia* (both built in 1938) and *Adinda* of 1939.

Under the Dutch flag typical movements of *Felipes* were from Pladju in 12th May 1951 for Bangkok, from Pulau Bukom on 11th October 1953 for Pladju, from Pladju on 20th November 1953 for Tjilatjap (modern Cilacap), and from Pulau Bukom on 21st December 1955 for Port Dickson. On 29th January 1956 she sailed from Pladju for Djakarta. During that year *Felipes* was transferred from Nederlandsche-Indies Tankstoomboot Maatschappij to 'La Corona', both part of the Royal Dutch Shell group. In October 1958 she was dry docked at Keppel Harbour, Singapore, and transferred from the Dutch to the British flag. However, the transfer did not go smoothly, and she needed to be registered at Singapore for a week whilst various survey items were clarified and documentation finalised. Under the British flag her tonnages rose to 3,052 gross and 1,666 net. Her destinations during the next few months included Pulau Bukom, Tanjung Priok (Djakarta), Surabaya, Tjilatjap, Balik Papen, Sorong, Belawan, Port Dickson, Port Swettenham and Penang. On 6th March 1963 she sailed from Pladju to Tjilatjap, and from Pulau Bukom on 26th April 1963 for Wyndham on the Ord River, Australia. She sailed from Pulau Bukom on 31st October 1963 to Pladju, and was reported on 8th November 1963

Felipes. [David Whiteside collection]

to be assisting the British tanker *Huntfield* (11,113/1953), which had gone aground in the Musi River, Palembang, Indonesia, and had been unable to refloat despite tug assistance. *Felipes* took 2,000 tons of cargo off *Huntfield* which enabled her to be refloated on 10th November. *Huntfield* was later dry docked in Hong Kong to repair damaged propeller blade tips and tail shaft wear. *Felipes* also made visits to Ma-Kharm Bay, Phuket, Thailand to discharge oil products from Pulau Bukom via a submarine pipeline. It was reported in December 1964 that *Felipes* had been sold to Singapore shipbreakers, but her exact date of arrival there is unknown.

TANEA

John Crown and Sons Ltd., Sunderland (Yard No. 231), 1950; 3,060g, 1,625n, 3,325d; 331.9 (o.a.) x 46.1 x 16.7 feet 6-cylinder 4SCSA Werkspoor-type oil engine by Hawthorn, Leslie and Co. Ltd., Newcastle-upon-Tyne, 333 NHP, 10.75 knots at 6.5 tons/day.

Tanea was launched on 17th May 1950 and completed on 25th July 1950 at a cost of £297,024. Registered at Wellington, she had six sets of port, centre and starboard cargo tanks, with numbers 4 centre and 6 centre designed for the dual carriage of bulk oil or case oil. They were fitted with large, removable, gastight hatches, and

Tanea. [Ships in Focus]

Tanea at Wanganui in 1963 or 1964, shortly before she left New Zealand waters. *[Ian J. Farquhar]*

flat metal guard plates were fitted to the internal pipelines to avoid damage from drummed cargo. Four two-ton derricks on the main mast served the two case oil tanks, and she had a trunk deck. *Tanea* was similar to *Felipes*, which preceded her from the same yard, the only external differences being the absence of derricks on the latter's mainmast (she did not need them as numbers 4 and 6 holds were not designed for dual use) and *Felipes* was not fitted with rubbing strakes on her hull, whereas *Tanea*, built for coastal trading, was fitted with rubbing strakes.

Tanea's delivery voyage began when she sailed from Sunderland on 27th July 1950 for New Zealand via Bari, Haifa, Port Said, Suez, Abadan, and Singapore. She arrived at Wellington on 22nd October 1950 and took up New Zealand coastal voyages previously carried out by *Paua* (1,412/1927). She carried refined oils, usually loading at Burnham Wharf, Wellington where petrol, diesel and kerosene had been discharged ashore into storage tanks by larger ocean-going tankers for redistribution to various New Zealand coastal oil depots. The opening of New Zealand Refining Company's Marsden Point refinery at Whangarei early in 1964 completely changed the coastal distribution pattern, and *Tanea* became too small for the work of carrying refined oils from the refinery around the coast. After dry docking in the floating dock at Wellington between 31st March and 2nd April 1964 she sailed from Wellington

for the last time on 17th April 1964 bound for Singapore. She had been transferred from Shell Company of New Zealand and Wellington registry to Shell Tankers (U.K.) Ltd. and London registry, for trading around the Singapore area.

In May 1965 *Tanea* worked in South Vietnamese waters, and between July 1965 and July 1967 regularly traded from Singapore to north west Australian ports such as Port Hedland and Broome, sometimes calling at Cocos Island part-loaded on the return trip. Between July and September 1967 she underwent extensive steel renewals at Jurong Dry Dock, Singapore, then between October 1967 and March 1968 served as a lightening tanker off South

Vietnam. She then reverted to trading between Singapore and north west Australian ports until September 1968, after which she worked almost exclusively in the Singapore area. She normally loaded at Port Dickson, Pulau Bukom, and sometimes Miri, for discharge at Woodlands on Singapore Island, Kuching, Phuket, Penang, Telok Anson, and also made one-off voyages to Cocos Island, Nha Trang, Da Nang, Labuan, and Kota Kinabalu in 1969. From 1970 she traded exclusively between Pulau Bukom and Woodlands until 20th January 1972 when she was laid up in the Western Anchorage, Singapore. She arrived at Jurong on 31st January 1972 and was handed over to shipbreakers on 2nd February.

Tanea. [Airfoto Malacca/Michael Pryce collection]

FRAGUM

Smith's Dock Co. Ltd., South Bank, Middlesbrough (Yard No. 1219), 1952; 2,926g, 1,280n, 3,416d, 331.9 (l.o.a.) x 46.4 x17.0 feet.
T.3-cyl. by Smith's Dock Co. Ltd., South Bank, Middlesbrough, 1,600 IHP, 11.5 knots.

Fragum was launched on 28th November 1951 and completed on 4th April 1952 at a cost of £333,771. Owners were the Anglo-Saxon Petroleum Co. Ltd. who registered her at London. She was designed to carry bitumen in six centre tanks, with ballast only in the wing tanks. The main trade for which she was intended was supplying bitumen from the Stanlow refinery to Ardrossan for the Scottish linoleum industry. She made her maiden voyage from Middlesbrough to Heysham, arriving on 9th April 1952, and sailing next day for Barton with fuel oil. She was mostly used in the west coast trade, loading bitumen in the Mersey for Ardrossan, then sailing southwards in ballast to Heysham to load fuel oil for discharge mainly at Ardrossan again, at Dingle on the Mersey, in the Manchester Ship Canal (at Barton, Cadishead, Ince, Mode Wheel or Stanlow), or Belfast or Dublin. A few voyages from Heysham were made to Old Kilpatrick on the Clyde with fuel oil. In December 1953 she became the largest vessel to visit the port of Ayr, where she was repaired by Ayr Engineering and Construction Co. Ltd. In quiet periods between bitumen cargoes she was used to carry fuel

Three views of *Fragum*, the bottom one at Swansea, and opposite top a starring role for her in an advertisement. *[Roy Fenton collection (3); Michael Pryce collection]*

oil but, when both trades were quiet, often laid-over in Herculaneum Dock, Liverpool. In the 'Journal of Commerce and Shipping Telegraph' of 16th March 1960 she was recorded as being in Number 4 Dock of Grayson Rollo and Clover Docks Ltd. undergoing refit and repairs. After hundreds of calls at Heysham, she arrived there for the last time from Ardrossan on 13th December 1963, loaded fuel oil for Old Kilpatrick then, after discharge, sailed through the Pentland Firth to a Tyne shipyard for refit and renaming. *Fragum* was replaced in the British coastal trade by the German bitumen tanker *Wangeroog* (999/1963), which arrived in ballast brand new at Heysham from Rendsburg on 17th December 1963 and, after loading fuel oil, sailed the same day for Ardrossan. Shell's Ardrossan installation had been acquired after the Second World War and converted from an aviation-fuel canning plant to a bitumen refinery. Later the Ardrossan depot was enlarged so that it could receive at Montgomerie Pier 18,000 tons deadweight tankers partly-laden with diesel, petrol and kerosene, some of which was redistributed to smaller Scottish ports in coastal tankers. Shell closed their Ardrossan depot in 1986.

At Newcastle-upon-Tyne *Fragum* was transferred to Shell Oil N.Z. Ltd., renamed *Maurea* and registered at Wellington. She was one of the first Shell tankers to receive the new funnel colours of red with a yellow shell. She arrived at Wellington on 9th April 1964 via Curacao and Panama, just eight days before *Tanea* left for Singapore. *Maurea* started a new coastal trade distributing bitumen and fuel oil from Marsden Point. However, she was eventually to prove too small for this trade and in August 1970

Maurea. [Ian J. Farquhar]

was replaced by the larger tanker *Erne* (13,728/1962). After a period of lay-up at Lyttelton she was sold on 17th April 1971 to Ocean Bitumen Carriers Inc., part of the C.Y. Tung group of companies, and was renamed *Dayu*, registered at Monrovia. *Dayu* sailed from New Zealand for the Far East and changed her funnel markings to those of her new owners: blue with a black top, with a yellow star. She was next reported working in the Saigon and Mekong Rivers, trades for which her size would suit her admirably, probably loading cargo at Hong Kong or Singapore, or transhipping cargo from tankers at Saigon. 'Lloyd's Shipping Index' noted her as trading between Pulau Bukom, Penang and Port Dickson in December 1973. She was observed in Singapore's Western Anchorage on 18th July 1975. At a time of rising fuel oil prices her triple-expansion steam engines were increasingly uneconomical, and she arrived at Hong Kong in March 1976 for demolition by Fuji, Marden and Co. Ltd.

Dayu. [Airfoto Malacca/J. and M. Clarkson]

SHELLPHALTE

John Crown and Sons Ltd., Sunderland (Yard No.234), 1952; 2,929g, 1,279n, 3,432d, 331.9 (l.o.a.) x 46.1 x 17.1 feet. T.3-cyl. by Smith's Dock Co. Ltd., South Bank-on-Tees, 1,800 IHP, 11.5 knots.
Shellphalte was launched on 27th March 1952 and completed on 16th July 1952 at a cost of £273.000. Two oil-fired Scotch boilers by Central Marine Engineering Works Ltd. produced steam at 220 psi. She was completed for Société Maritime Shell, Paris, and was registered at Le Havre. *Shellphalte* was designed as a bitumen tanker, and could discharge cargo at a rate of 360 tons per hour. She had a trunk deck and a considerable amount of welding was used in her construction. Her cargo space was divided into six centre cargo tanks and 12 wing ballast tanks, with a cargo pump room sited between numbers 3 and 4 tanks. Accommodation for the deck officers was provided on the bridge deck, for her master on the navigating bridge, for the engine-room officers and petty officers in a house on the boat deck aft, and for the seamen, firemen and caterers on the poop deck either side of the machinery casing. Recorded movements included sailing from Port de Bouc (west of Marseilles) on 11th October 1953 for Algiers, and sailing from Algiers on 23rd November 1953 for Port de Bouc. She was sold in 1963 to 'Soflumar' (Société d'Armement Fluvial et Maritime) and renamed *Port Blanc*, registered at Dunkirk, and with her tonnages re-measured as 2,950 gross, 1,438 net tons but still of 3,432 tons deadweight. She was sold again in 1972 and renamed *Ragno* by Societa Siciliana di Navigazione per Azioni SO. SI. NA, Italy. In 1973 she went to Danaos Shipping

Shellphalte. [Michael Pryce collection]

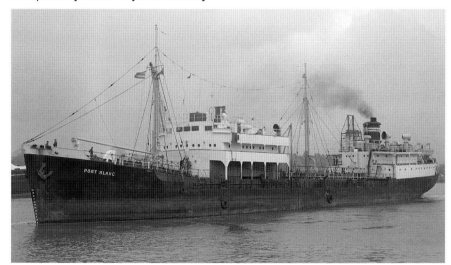

Port Blanc at Preston. [J. and M. Clarkson]

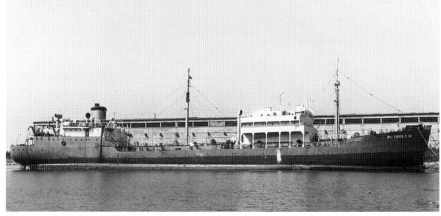

Petrola 12. [Michael Pryce collection]

Two views of *Irish Holly,* above assisted by Alexandra tugs as she approaches the locks at Eastham. *[J. and M. Clarkson (2)]*

and Trading Corporation (John S. Latsis, Piraeus, manager) and was renamed *Petro Asphalt I,* becoming *Petrola XII* in 1974 and *Petrola 12* in 1976. By that time her tonnages were 2,928 gross and 1,149 net. Sold to Greek shipbreakers she was lying at Eleusis, Piraeus awaiting demolition on 28th September 1982.

IRISH HOLLY

William Gray and Co. Ltd., West Hartlepool (Yard No. 1279), 1954; 2,940g, 1,381n, 3,350d, 330.1 (l.o.a.) x 46.2 x 17.3
T.3-cyl. by Smith's Dock Co. Ltd., South Bank, Middlesbrough, 11 knots.
Irish Holly was ordered as a 3,150-ton deadweight tanker as part of a building programme for Irish Shipping Ltd. initiated on 1st November 1951 under a guarantee from the Irish Government. She was completed on 6th May 1954 and registered at Dublin. The only other tankers ever owned by Irish Shipping Ltd. were the larger 12,168 gross *Irish Hawthorn* and *Irish Blackthorn,* built in 1958 and 1959 respectively by Fairfield Ship Building and Engineering Co. Ltd., Govan, and very similar, although not identical, to Shell's 18,000-deadweight H-class. *Irish Holly* was very similar to *Fragum* and *Shellphalte,* but the major visible difference was that she had the sides of her poop plated-in, thereby providing more sheltered accommodation space. Amidships, the middle-upper part of her accommodation was also plated-in, but she still retained the open sides and centre castle bulkheads perforated to allow heat to escape. However, *Irish Holly* mainly carried white oil cargoes such as diesel, and not bitumen. Her funnel was also taller than those of the two Shell steam tankers.

Originally, *Irish Holly* traded mainly from the Dublin oil depot. Her first arrival at Heysham was from Belfast on 11th October 1957, loading diesel and sailing for Dublin the next day. Over the next 12 years she made a total of 110 visits to Heysham, arriving every few weeks on average, usually from Belfast, Dublin or Limerick, and always loading diesel, usually for Dublin or Belfast. She also occasionally loaded diesel at Heysham for Old Kilpatrick, Ardrossan, Faslane, the Manchester Ship Canal berths, or Dingle on the Mersey.

In June 1957 it was decided to build an oil refinery in Ireland. The Irish Refining Company Ltd. was a consortium of the Californian Texas Oil Corporation, Esso Petroleum Co. Ltd. and Shell Mex and BP Ltd. The refinery was to supply an expanding domestic market which was expected to consume enough petroleum products to justify the capital needed to establish the operation. Located at Whitegate, County Cork, the refinery had a capacity of two million tonnes per annum. When Irish Refining Co. Ltd. completed their refinery and jetty on Corkbeg Island, on one side of

the bay at Whitegate, *Irish Holly* was the first tanker to discharge there on 7th April 1959 and she made many calls at Whitegate thereafter.

Her other recorded movements included sailing from Old Kilpatrick on the Clyde on 14th March 1960 to Faslane, at Ardrossan on 27th April 1962, and she was observed at Stanlow on 6th August 1965, 13th August 1965 and 2nd August 1965. She was sold in July 1967 to A.N.A.P.O. Compagnia de Navigazione Bunkeraggi S.p.A., Italy, and renamed *Etnea,* but was destined to have but a short career under that name. On 7th January 1968 when moored at a breakwater in the port of Vibo Valentia her moorings broke during a storm and she went on to rocks, to be abandoned on 10th January. She was refloated on 22nd April 1968 with the assistance of tugs and pontoons and was moored in Vibo Valentia for survey, but was found to be beyond economical repair. She arrived in tow at La Spezia on 12th June 1968. On 7th August 1968 she was sold by underwriters to S.p.A. Cantieri Navale 'Santa Maria' of Genoa for demolition at their yard at La Spezia.

Tankers and builders

A noticeable difference between the two motor and three steam tankers was that the former had their funnels towards the aft end of their aft accommodation whereas the three steam tankers had their funnels sited towards the forward end of their aft accommodation.

The five tankers were all built by British shipyards that have since closed. John Crown and Sons Ltd., who built three, was swallowed-up in a 1960 reorganisation by Joseph L. Thompson, when they built their North Sands yard on land formerly occupied by the neighbouring Crown shipyard. The North Sands yard ceased shipbuilding after 1979 and was placed on a care-and-maintenance basis until reactivated in 1986 for the construction of a large crane barge for North Sea oil work. After this was completed in 1987 the yard was closed, demolished and levelled for housing and redevelopment.

Smith's Dock Co. Ltd., South Bank ceased shipbuilding in 1987. William Gray and Co. Ltd. went into voluntary liquidation in 1962. Irish Shipping Ltd. was placed into liquidation in 1984. Shell are still a major oil company, with shipping and oil trading arms merged in 1995 as Shell International Trading and Shipping Co. (STASCO). The familiar shell emblem disappeared from their funnels in 1998, replaced by a plain buff funnel with a black top, which is how they were before the shell was first displayed on funnels in 1946. Although Shell still operates a large fleet, the majority of its ships are large, managed LNG carriers or chartered tankers. Excepting the LNG carriers, tankers are still given the latin names of shells, but the bland funnel devoid of the shell emblem does not make them obviously recognisable.

The five tankers met various fates. Built to an old-fashioned design, they were soon competing with more modern tankers which had smaller crews, reduced steelwork (no amidships accommodation) and more efficient diesel engines. *Felipes* was effectively a larger member of Shell's Eastern Fleet trading around the Singapore area, which had been supplemented after the Second World War by former Empire tankers given similar names beginning with the letter F. *Tanea* was built for a niche coastal trade in New Zealand, after which she followed *Felipes* out east when replaced by *Fragum*. The French-flag *Shellphalte* was built to handle Société Maritime Shell's long-standing bitumen trade to North Africa, but Algeria was declared independent from France in July 1962 and elected its first president in 1963. Following the disruption of Algeria's society and economy when European French managers and skilled workers left the country, all industrial and commercial properties previously owned by Europeans were confiscated in March 1963, and it was probably this that ended her Algerian bitumen trade and resulted in her sale later in 1963. *Irish Holly* was sold after a career of only 13 years, so had obviously become surplus to requirements, and it is likely that her triple-expansion steam engine and large crew made her uneconomical in comparison with newer and more efficient coastal ships. Additionally, by the 1960s, larger 18,000-tonnes-deadweight tankers were being used by the major oil companies for coastal oil distribution.

This photograph is believed to have been taken when *Tanea* was laid up in Western Anchorage, Singapore, in January 1972, shortly before she was scrapped. She has her windsails rigged to gas-free her cargo tanks. *Tanea* was never used at Singapore as a bunkering tanker, but ran between Pulau Bukom refinery and Shell's Woodlands depot (near the Causeway at Singapore) with refined oils. She was not fitted with heating coils and so could not carry the heavier fuel oils used for bunkering.
[V. H. Young/Ships in Focus collection]

A HISTORY OF BARBER LINES A/S
Malcolm Cranfield

The Norwegian company Barber Lines A/S was formed in 1969 by Wilh. Wilhelmsen, Fearnley & Eger and A.F. Klaveness to serve cargo liner trades based on the United States of America at a time when containerisation was in its infancy. The Line's general agents in the United States were Barber Steamship Lines Inc.

This article traces the origins of Barber Lines A/S and the associated Barber Blue Sea Line, the origins of which have, besides the Norwegian companies listed above, involved shipping companies from the United States, Hong Kong, Sweden, the Philippines and the United Kingdom.

Barber Steamship Lines
Barber Steamship Lines was the first line to operate scheduled services between New York and the Far East via Suez. It was created in 1893 by shipping agents and charterers Barber and Co., a partnership between English brothers Herbert and James Barber who had settled at Englewood, New Jersey. Even as late as 1985, the Chairman of Barber Steamship was one of James Barber's descendents, Ed Barber.

The Barber brothers had originally been employed in England by Patton, Vickers and Co. of Liverpool, a company which had traded with the United States employing sailing ships such as the *North Carolina*, a 205-foot iron-hulled barque built at Dumbarton in 1876. This ship was lost on New Year's Day 1880 after grounding on Bermuda's western reefs during a voyage from Baltimore to Liverpool with a cargo of cotton and other goods. Herbert Barber was at that time based in New York as owners' representative.

Barber and Co. was established in 1883 with Herbert Barber in New York while James Barber remained in London until emigrating to the United States in 1887. Major expansion took place during 1901 and 1902 when the business was incorporated as Barber and Co. Inc. A service using sailing ships was inaugurated between North America and Europe, with branch offices opened at Norfolk (Virginia), Liverpool and London. The New York and Oriental Steamship Co. Ltd. was established in Liverpool to purchase new vessels and operate them between New York and the Far East.

The New York and Oriental Steamship Co. Ltd. commenced trading with sister ships *Satsuma* and *Shimosa*, built by Short Brothers at Sunderland in 1901 and 1902, to which was later added *Suruga*, built by McMillan at Dumbarton in 1908. The ships were managed from Barber and Co.'s office in Alexandra Buildings, Liverpool, in association with local owner Barnett. A Vincent G. Barnett had, on the death of

James Barber's son Edward J. Barber, become chairman of Barber Steamship in 1953. He retired in 1963 when Ed Barber added this role to his existing duties as president.

In 1907 the La Plata Steamship Co. Ltd. was created to operate chartered steamers between New York and the east coast of South America, a service started by Barber in 1904. A 1911 sailing list shows that Barber and Co. Inc. operated chartered ships to the River Plate while marketing the services of Clan Line to France, Union-Castle to South Africa and, most significantly, a service to the Far East provided by the Lancashire Shipping Company with their *Muncaster Castle*. The last-named company, originally the Lancaster Shipowners Company, was formed in 1896 and managed by James Chambers and Co. of Liverpool.

On the outbreak of the First World War in 1914 *Satsuma* and *Suruga* were transferred to the United States' flag and placed under the direct management of Barber and Co. Inc., which also took over the marketing of the New York and Oriental Steamship Company's services. The ships were sold in 1924 and 1925, *Satsuma* foundering in 1929 while *Suruga* was scuttled at Normandy on 9th June 1944. Herbert Barber died in 1915 and James Barber two years later, succeeded as president by Edward J. Barber. The outbreak of war had also required the direct business relationship between Barber and Barnett to be split, so that *Shimosa* was exchanged for Barnett's *Dochra*, built by Swan Hunter in 1906. *Dochra* was subsequently operated to the River Plate by Barber's La Plata Steamship Co. Ltd. until her sale in 1925. *Shimosa* became a war casualty in 1917 whilst *Dochra* was lost as the Italian *Capo Vado* in 1940.

The return service from the Far East to the United States was known as the Dodwell-Castle Line. Dodwell and Co., who had acted as Barber's Far East agents, was formed in Shanghai in 1858 and was established as a

Seen in Italian ownership receiving temporary hull repairs, *Capo Vado* was built in 1906 as *Dochra* for Barnett of Liverpool and was transferred in 1914 to Barber Steamship Lines for the South American services of La Plata Steam Ship Co. Ltd. Sold to Italy in 1926, *Capo Vado* was sunk by Royal Navy cruisers off Albania in November 1940. *[Newall Dunn collection]*

British company in 1899. In 1905 Barber and Dodwell had participated in the creation of shipping pools to control capacity and freight rates and in 1912 the 'New York Times' reported that these arrangements were under challenge by the United States Government as being contrary to the Sherman Antitrust Act of 1890. James and Herbert Barber were among those named. Further demonstrating the high profile of Barber in the United States maritime business community, a 1907 report in the 'New York Times', concerning anti-trust action against Standard Oil in the trade to South Africa, had named a George Barber as agent for 'Union Clan Line', being one of the Lines involved. This reference, together with Barber's marketing activity as described above, indicates an interesting early link between Union-Castle Mail Steamship Company, formed on 8th March 1900 with the merger of Union Line and Donald Currie's Castle Shipping Line, and Clan Line which had extended its services to North America.

Barber Steamship Lines was incorporated in 1917 and developed as a freight sales organisation when the United States Shipping Board awarded it the management of the United States to West Africa trade route. This route employed seven state-owned ships built between 1918 and 1920: *Cathlamet*, *Otho*, *Padnsay*, *West Humhaw*, *West Irmo*, *West Kebar* and *Zarembo*. In 1928 Barber brought the trade route and the seven ships into its private ownership, creating the American West African Line Inc., with Barber Steamship appointed managers. One ship, *Padnsay*, was sold in 1938 while four of the ships were lost in 1942 and only two survived the Second World War, *Cathlamet* and *Zarembo*, both being sold in 1947 and the service thereafter was tonnaged by Norwegian ships. Barber West African Line was created in 1931 and barges were operated under its name at Lagos, Nigeria. Two remained in service until at least 1947.

The Norwegian connection

The Norwegian shipping company Wilh. Wilhelmsen, involved with Barber Steamship for many years through its interest in A. N. Hansen and Co. of Copenhagen, had in November 1927 embarked on a major new venture. Together with the Lancashire Shipping Company's Castle Line (formerly the Dodwell-Castle Line), Wilhelmsen reached agreement for each to employ five ships on Barber Steamship Line's service between New York and the Far East, the ships to wear Barber funnel colours. This joint service was enhanced in 1929 by the creation of a new Barber Wilhelmsen Line to serve the homebound trade from the Far East to the east coast of the United States via Panama. In order to provide sufficient capacity for both services, ten almost identical motor liners designed for carrying vegetable oil and reefer cargo were built by Wilhelmsen between 1928 and 1930. Five of the ships were given Chinese names with the prefix *Tai*. *Tai Yang* was the first, *Troja* the last of the ten ships. However, Barber Wilhelmsen Line services ceased for the duration of the Second World War.

Records for the five *Tai* ships on the Norwegian website www.warsailors.com show that, when Norway was invaded by Germany on 9th April 1940, *Tai Yin* was in Fremantle, having arrived from Melbourne the previous day intending to load for Oslo, and *Tai Ping Yang* was on her way from Casablanca to Queenstown (Cobh), Eire. *Tai Shan* had arrived at Gothenburg on 20th March 1940 with a cargo for the RAF, escaping to the United Kingdom on 23rd January 1941 together with *Elizabeth Bakke*, *John Bakke*, *Taurus* and *Ranja*. *Tai Yang* had departed Padang on 2nd April 1940, arriving London on 29th May, while *Tai Ping* had been captured by the Germans and was scuttled at Gironde on 26th August 1944 as *Sperrbrecher 14*.

Also in April 1940, the Norwegian Shipping and

The 15-knot *Tai Yin*, built by Deutsche Werke at Kiel in 1929 and photographed arriving at Oslo around 1960, was one of ten new ships built to serve both Wilhelmsen's outbound joint service with Barber Steamship Lines/Lancashire Shipping Company and also the new homebound Barber Wilhelmsen Line service from the Far East to the east coast of the United States via Panama. *Tai Yin* was broken up at Osaka in August 1961. *[Per-Erik Johnsen/Malcolm Cranfield collection]*

Fearnley & Eger's *Ferngrove* was built at Greaker, Norway in 1950, and was photographed in Barber Steamship colours at Boston in January 1961. In 1964 she was sold to Haugesund owners and renamed *Notos,* later sailing under the Cyprus flag until broken up at Sachana in 1981. *[Earl G.Boyd/James Bartke collection]*

had cooperated from 1910 to 1920), had in 1925 commenced a long-lasting relationship with A.F. Klaveness. This company had begun in business at Sandefjord in 1898 but had moved to Lysaker (near Oslo) in 1910. Both Fearnley & Eger and A.F. Klaveness provided new ships for the Fern Line service between United States Gulf and Pacific coast ports and Japan and China. When cooperation resumed after the Second World War, the service was renamed Fern-Ville Lines and on the return leg commenced calling at Venezuelan ports.

In January 1948 Barber Wilhelmsen Line joined with Fern-Ville Lines to create Barber-Fern-Ville Lines on the homebound trade to the Gulf of Mexico and the east coast of the United States. As they loaded cargo in different areas of the

Trade Mission (Nortraship) was established in London to administer the Norwegian merchant fleet outside German controlled areas and Wilhelmsen agreed with Nortraship to have several of their modern liner vessels allocated into the East Coast United States - West African service, managed by Barber Steamship. This arrangement was extended in 1946 into a joint venture named Barber West African Line with three vessels supplied by Wilhelmsen, together with two from Fearnley & Eger and A.F. Klaveness, which was later increased to three when Barber Steamship sold their last vessel. The ships latterly employed had included the 1950-built *Ferngrove,* the 1957-built *Fernwood,* 1958-built *Titania* and 1959-built *Fernwave,* all photographed with Barber Steamship funnel markings.

Fearnley & Eger, who had started business in Oslo in 1872 (just a few years after Wilhelmsen with whom they

United States, the two groups' interests continued to operate independently outbound and Klaveness retained an entirely separate service between the Pacific coast and South East Asia.

Barber Steamship Lines had meanwhile been appointed by Fearnley & Eger as sales agent for their service to the Mediterranean and Levant from the Atlantic coast of the United States and after 1957 from Gulf ports. In 1963 this service was joined by DFDS of Copenhagen, becoming Nordana Line, but Fearnley & Eger withdrew the following year.

Mollers of Hong Kong
The agreements between Barber Steamship, Wilhelmsen and the Lancashire Shipping Company's Castle Line were renewed in December 1945. However, the Castle Line fleet

The motor vessel *Raby Castle* was built at Dundee in 1925 for the Lancashire Shipping Co. Ltd. In 1943 she was sold to J.A. Billmeir and Co.

Ltd. who renamed her *Stanhall* once Government regulations were relaxed in 1945. She became Wallem's *Ami* in 1951, and the Japanese *Hisakawa*

Maru in 1956, and was demolished at Osaka in 1962. *[J. and M. Clarkson collection]*

had been depleted by the loss of the 1928-built *Muncaster Castle*, torpedoed in March 1942, and by the sale to Stanhope Shipping in 1943 of the 1925-built *Raby Castle*, which became *Stanhall*.

In October 1944 Mollers of Hong Kong had bought a controlling interest in James Chambers and Co. and appointed themselves managers of the Lancashire Shipping Company. In 1946 Mollers proceeded to sell Castle Line's remaining three ships, *Greystoke Castle*, *Thurland Castle* and *Penrith Castle*, all built by Cammell Laird during 1929, to Elder Dempster Lines, who renamed them *Freetown*, *Fulani* and *Fantee* respectively.

In 1947, in order to meet Mollers' tonnage commitment for the Castle Line joint service with Barber Steamship and Wilhelmsen, a newly created subsidiary, Moller Line (UK) Ltd., purchased two C3-S-A1 type ships built at Seattle-Tacoma in 1943 as USS *Willapa* and USS *Perdito*. These had entered service in 1944 as the British escort carriers HMS *Puncher* and HMS *Trouncer* and had been returned to the United States Navy early in 1946. Although contracts were placed at Baltimore for their conversion into cargo liners, delays arose due to a shortage of steel and the *Muncaster Castle* and *Greystoke Castle* did not enter service until 1948.

Meanwhile three ships building for the Lancashire Shipping Company (two of which were ordered from Blyth Drydock and Shipbuilding Company which was also owned by Mollers) were also delayed and two were sold on the stocks in 1950. In 'Sold East' Howard Dick and Stephen Kentwell record that the reasons for this sale included the weakness of the Japanese economy and the Communist takeover of China, both making for bleak trading prospects, although trade subsequently improved during the 1952-1954 Korean War. Statements in an article by John McRoberts, published in 'Sea Breezes' in 1973, that Mollers had considered that 'the old round the world Dodwell-Castle Line service was virtually finished', and 'it was only a matter of time before they would have been forced to give up the service', help explain Mollers' withdrawal from the service.

Penrith Castle, built at Blyth in 1949, in fact served the Lancashire Shipping Company for almost three years before being sold to Ben Line in 1952 to become *Benmhor*. In 1954 the modified C3s were chartered out for five years to Shaw Savill and Albion to become *Bardic* and *Gallic* respectively. Later they were also purchased by Ben Line to become *Bennevis* and *Benrinnes*.

The two ships sold on the stocks were to have been named *Bolton Castle*, built by A. Stephen at Glasgow and delivered in 1950 to Blue Star Line as *Dunedin Star*, and *Thurland Castle*, delivered at Blyth to the Pacific Steam Navigation Co. Ltd. in 1951 as *Cuzco* and sold to Ben Line in 1965 to become *Benattow*.

Reflecting Mollers' short post-war involvement with Barber Wilhemsen, in 1977 the Castle Line naming policy was revived with the building in Japan of a new *Muncaster Castle*. Together with the *Merry Viking* of sister company Redfern Shipping, she had been ordered for the short-lived Hongkong International Container Line, a four-ship joint venture with Thai Marine to serve the trade between the Pacific Coast and the Far East, which collapsed in 1981.

Mollers had also sought involvement in the Pacific Orient Express Line, jointly operated after 1948 by the Norwegian Ditlev-Simonsen and the Transatlantic Line of Sweden. Thus, in April 1947 four Liberty ships, which were named *Lilian Moller*, *Mary Moller*, *Norah Moller* and *Rosalie Moller*, were purchased for the service. However, in March 1948 all were sold to T. and J. Harrison of Liverpool.

Barber Lines A/S

Wilhelmsen, Fearnley & Eger and Klaveness together created Barber Lines A/S in September 1969 and pooled the majority of their remaining dry cargo vessels as in the list on page 50. They were painted in a dramatic new colour scheme of orange hull, pale green superstructure and two large vertical orange stripes on a black funnel. The World Ship Society's history of Wilhemsen notes that 'exterior beauty and company individuality were sacrificed for easier maintenance and a new common image'. While the orange hull colour became closer to red and, as green was a disaster to maintain that colour was quickly phased out, the inverted orange stripes on the funnel remain unique. Barber Steamship continued as general agents in the United States for Barber Lines A/S.

Barber Middle East Line, created in 1964 to serve the trade between the United States and the Red Sea/Arabian Gulf, was expanded in 1969 through the purchase of Van Nievelt & Goudriaan's Constellation Line, together with its four vessels. New ro-ro vessels were introduced in 1979 to this service which had been highly successful until the outbreak of the Iran-Iraq War in 1979 caused the collapse of trade to the Middle East.

Wilhelmsen took full ownership of Barber Lines A/S in 1975, chartering in the vessels until then contributed by Fearnley & Eger (*Fernmoor*, *Fernstate*, *Fernview* and *Fernlake*) and by Klaveness (*Kingsville* and *Queensville*). *Fernmoor* was sold early in 1975 and *Fernstate* in 1976.

Fearnley & Eger's *Fernview*, built at Gothenburg in 1961, was photographed at Vancouver in August 1973 after being lengthened and painted in Barber Lines A/S colours. She was sold to Wilhelmsen in 1976 and, renamed *Texas*, continuing in Barber Lines A/S service until sold to Saudi in 1982. *[Malcolm Cranfield collection]*

Fearnley & Eger's *Fernmoor*, built at Scotstoun in 1955, was photographed at Vancouver in May 1972 in the colours of Barber Lines A/S which she served from 1969 until early 1975 (above). *[Malcolm Cranfield collection]* Wihelmsen's *Tijuca,* built by Connell at Glasgow in 1959, served Barber Lines A/S from 1969 to 1977 (right). *[Malcolm Cranfield collection]* Wilhelmsen's *Traviata*, built at Hamburg in 1959 and lengthened in 1970, served in Barber Lines A/S colours from 1969 to 1979 and was photographed in June 1976 (below). She was soon renamed *Tema* under the nominal ownership of Arctic Shipping, Singapore. *[Malcolm Cranfield collection]*

Ships on Barber Lines A/S services

Wilhelmsen

Titania (ex *Crestville*) of 1958 and *Tema* (ex *Brookville*) of 1960, purchased in 1961 and 1963 respectively, served Barber West African Line until their sale in 1971.
Themis, *Tugela* and *Toreador*, built in 1954, *Turandot*, built 1957, and *Tijuca*, built 1959; *Tampa*, *Tortugas*, *Texas* and *Tennessee*, built 1959/60 acquired with Constellation Line but sold to China in 1973.
Temeraire, *Tagaytay*, *Tai Ping*, *Traviata* and *Tarantel*, all built between 1957 and 1960, and *Taronga*, *Tamerlane*, *Tirranna* and *Taimyr*, all built in 1967 or 1968. These were all lengthened in 1970 and 1971, given new 'midships sections and fitted for container stowage and handling. *Traviata* was renamed *Tema* in 1977.
The 1953-built *Tagus* and *Theben* joined the Barber Lines A/S fleet in about 1972, *Tagus* reverting to Wilhelmsen service and funnel colours by early 1974. The 1968-built

Trinidad, *Taiko* and *Talabot* joined the fleet in 1973. Ships on charter included the German *Mangan* (renamed *Barber Mangan*) from 1970 to 1972, Ben Line's *Benstac* from 1973 to 1978 and briefly Strick Line's *Shahristan*.

Fearnley & Eger

Fernbank, *Fernbrook*, *Ferncliff*, *Ferngate*, *Fernlake*, *Fernland*, *Fernmoor*, *Fernstate*, *Fernview* and *Fernwave*. *Fernbrook* and *Ferngate* were sold in 1973 with a charter back until 1974/75, being renamed *Barberbrook* and *Barbergate* for operation on the Barber West African Line.

Klaveness

Bonneville, *Bougainville*, *Bronxville*, *Corneville*, *Kingsville*, *Queensville*, *Roseville* and *Sunnyville*. In 1970 *Fernlake*, *Fernview*, *Kingsville* and *Queensville* were lengthened and given new 'midships sections fitted for container stowage and handling.

Wilhelmsen's *Theben*, built by Eriksbergs at Gothenburg in 1953, which had briefly served Barber Lines A/S between about 1972 to 1975, was photographed arriving at Vancouver in August 1974 in Barber Lines colours (above). In 1975 *Theben* was transferred to Arctic Shipping, Singapore. *[Steve Klassen/Dave Salisbury collection]*

Kingsville, built for A.F. Klaveness by Lithgows at Glasgow in 1956, was photographed at San Francisco in July 1974 after being lengthened in 1970 to provide a dedicated container stowage and handling section (right). She served Barber Lines A/S from 1969 until sold in 1977 and renamed *Sea Union*. She arrived at Kaohsiung in December 1978 to be broken up. *[Malcolm Cranfield collection]*

The lengthened, diesel-engined *Fern-lake* and *Fernview* were purchased by Wilhelmsen later in 1976 and renamed *Tampa* and *Texas* respectively, while the Klaveness steamers were sold in 1977 and soon scrapped.

On termination of the charters of *Barberbrook* and *Barbergate*, Barber West African Line had in 1975 briefly employed *Fernstate*, then *Tijuca* and *Tugela*, followed on their sale in 1976 and 1977 by *Taimyr* and *Tema* (ex *Traviata*). In 1980 these were replaced by *Tampa* (ex *Fernlake*) and *Texas* (ex *Fernview*) until they were sold in 1982. In 1983 and 1984 came the new ro-ros *Takoradi* and *Tema* chartered from Sekihyo Line.

Doña Nati, built at Nagasaki in 1951, was one of three ships delivered to the National Development Co. Inc. of Manila and bareboat chartered to De La Rama Lines. In 1957 Philippine National Lines took over management of the ships which were replaced in 1960 by the new 'President' class vessels from Japanese yards. *Doña Nati* was broken up at Kaohsiung in 1970. *[Malcolm Cranfield collection]*

Barber Blue Sea Line

In order to best serve niche ports and cargoes not then penetrated by containerisation, a new joint venture between Barber Lines A/S and Blue Sea Line was created at the end of 1974, logically named Barber Blue Sea Line. Blue Sea Line then comprised Blue Funnel Line of Liverpool and Swedish East Asia Company of Gothenburg, but it originated in 1940 in a partnership between the Swedish line and a Philippine company, as outlined below.

Barber West African Line was excluded from Barber Blue Sea Line, as was Barber Middle East Line until 1979 when all three partners contributed new ro-ro ships, followed by others in 1984. New multi-purpose ships were introduced in 1977 by both Wilhelmsen and Blue Funnel.

Blue Sea Line - De La Rama of the Philippines

In 1940 the De La Rama Steam Ship Co. Inc. linked up with the Swedish East Asia Company to operate a trans-Pacific service which later became known as the De La Rama round-the-world service. As a joint service between the Swedish company and Blue Funnel Line, this was from 1964 known as the Blue Sea Line.

The De La Rama Steam Ship Co. Inc. had been created by the De La Rama family of Iloilo who had participated in Philippine inter-island trading from the early 1900s. In September 1938 the steam ship company began a partnership with Ivaran Lines of Oslo, operators of four motor ships built in Sweden between 1936 and 1939, concluding with *Reinholt* which served Ivaran until 1965. For this new joint service, De La Rama ordered from the 'San Marco' shipyard of C.R.D.A. (Cantieri Riuniti dell'Adriatico) in Trieste three twin-screw motor ships, *Doña Aurora*, *Doña Aniceta* and *Doña Nati*. Registered at Manila, the ships flew the US flag until 1946 when they raised the Philippine flag following the granting of full independence from the United States Commonwealth. *Doña Aurora* was mined in 1942, becoming the subject of a lengthy legal dispute with the United States Government.

During the Second World War the Ivaran ships were necessarily dedicated to wartime duties. www. warsailors.com records that, on 23rd April 1942, during a voyage from Santos, Brazil to New York with a cargo of hides, *Reinholt* was shelled continuously for 20 minutes by *U 752*. The incident received much publicity on her arrival in New York and 15 men later received the Krigsmedaljen while the captain received the higher ranked Krigskorset. *Reinholt* sailed in trans-Atlantic convoys between the United States and United Kingdom for much of the remainder of the War.

De la Rama meanwhile chartered in neutral Swedish ships, a step which Ivaran regarded as a contravention of the terms of their agreement, leading to a break between the two companies. Suspended in 1942 once the United States had entered the war, following its

De La Rama's twin-screw motor ship *Dona Aniceta* was sold in 1950, becoming Polish Ocean Lines' *General Bem*, as seen on the Kiel Canal on 13th July 1969 bound for Khorramshahr. *[Malcolm Cranfield]*

resumption in 1946 the De La Rama-Seaco joint service was extended to cover east coast United States ports, with Ivaran Lines in direct competition.

Early in 1947 De La Rama introduced the C1-B type *Cape Constance*, renamed *Doña Trinidad,* which was wrecked in June that year, and *Cape Sandy*, renamed *Doña Aurora*. They further upgraded their fleet in 1950. The 1939-built *Doña Aniceta* (sold to Polish Ocean Lines and renamed *General Bem*) and *Doña Nati* (sold to Mitsui Sempaku of Japan and renamed *Asahisan Maru*), and also the 1943-built *Doña Aurora*, were replaced with new, bareboat-chartered ships named *Doña Alicia*, *Doña Aurora* and *Doña Nati*, built at Nagasaki in 1950 and 1951 under reparations arrangements and delivered to the Philippines Government-owned National Development Company of Manila.

However, in preparation for Japanese yards delivering a series of six 'President' ships in 1960 and 1961, the Philippine Government decided in 1957 that the country's interests were better served by withdrawing the three ships from De La Rama management and joining up again with Ivaran, albeit briefly, creating a state-owned marketing organisation to operate the three ships. This was initially named Philippine National Line ('PNL') and later United Philippine Lines ('UPL'),

On its incorporation in 1966 UPL acquired *Doña Nati* (scrapped in 1970) together with the six 'President' ships, all of which were sold in 1978 to newly created companies. Galleon Shipping Corporation of Manila acquired four, with the other two going to the Egyptian International Shipping Corporation, managed by Uiterwijk. *Doña Alicia* and *Doña Aurora* were meanwhile transferred in 1965 to the Maritime Company of the Philippines, a division of Compania Maritima, which operated competing services with similar ships to the 'President' class, renaming them *Lingayen Gulf* and *Sarangani Bay* respectively. They were scrapped during 1973.

Swedish East Asia Company ('Seaco')

A/B Svenska Ostasiatiska Kompaniet (Swedish East Asia Company, 'Seaco'), founded at Gothenburg in 1907 by Dan Broström, was by the late 1930s well established in the trades between Europe, the Indian subcontinent and the Far East. For these services and the new joint service with De La Rama, Seaco had ordered new vessels from Swedish yards which were delivered between 1940 to 1946 as *Bali*, *Mindoro*, *Mangalore*, *Bengal*, *Tonghai* (launched 1940 but not commissioned until 1944), *Travancore*, *Bataan* and *Andaman*.

In 1972 the Blue Sea Line services were upgraded and extended outbound from the United States to Australia by incorporating Seaco's Atlantrafik Express service. To this service, Blue Funnel Line contributed sister ships *Phemius* (ex *Glenfinlas*), *Perseus* (ex *Radnorshire*), *Phrontis* (ex *Pembrokeshire*) and *Patroclus* (ex *Glenalmond*) which all carried Seaco funnel colours until 1974.

On the creation of Barber Blue Sea Line in 1974, Seaco and sister company Malmros initially contributed three new ships, *Nagara*, *Tamara* and *Malmros Monsoon*. These served the homebound trade from the Far East to the United States, sailing outbound to Australia on Atlantrafik Express which had reverted to operation as an independent Seaco service.

A new ro-ro vessel, *Barber Nara*, was delivered in 1979 for dedicated Barber Blue Sea Line service. She wore the funnel colours of Broström A/B, the parent company of Seaco.

Ocean Transport and Trading plc (Blue Funnel)

Alfred Holt's Blue Funnel Line had entered the trade between China, Vancouver, Seattle, North Pacific Coast ports and San Diego in 1902 on acquisition of the China Mutual Steam Navigation Company. Following the acquisition of Indra Line in 1915, Blue Funnel also traded between New York and Far East ports via Panama, returning from Java to New York.

Mangalore was completed at Gothenburg for Seaco in 1943, and after the Second World War is understood to have worked on the joint service with De La Rama. Sold in 1969, she carried the names *Pierreangelaemme* and *Alwady* until broken up at Gadani Beach in 1977. *[J. and M. Clarkson collection]*

Teucer, built by J.L. Thompson in 1950 and launched at Sunderland as *Silverlaurel*, photographed sailing from Boston, was one of three new ships ordered by Silver Line for operation on their joint U.S.-based services with Prince Line but sold on the stocks to Blue Funnel Line for a competing new joint venture with De La Rama. For conference reasons she was placed under the Dutch flag. In 1960 *Teucer* was transferred to the British flag and as *Telamon* served Blue Sea Line until her sale in 1971. She traded briefly as *Aegis Epic* until broken up in 1972. *[William Schell/ Malcolm Cranfield collection]*

Blue Funnel Line's 1935 sailing list for their service between the Pacific coast and the Far East is included here. Dodwell & Co. were their agents on the Pacific coast of the United States and Canada.

Blue Funnel sailings October 1935-April 1936 (issued 20th October 1935)	
Vessels	**Ports of call**
Ixion *Talthybius* *Tyndareus* *Tantalus* (one round-trip voyage only)	Hong Kong, Miike (except *Tantalus*), Kobe, Nagoya, Yokohama, Victoria, Vancouver, Seattle, Tacoma. Return voyages: Tacoma, Seattle, Vancouver, Yokohama, Kobe, Miike (except *Tantalus*), Shanghai, Hong Kong.

In 1946 and 1947 six Victory-type ships were purchased from the United States Maritime Commission. A letter in the World Ship Society's journal 'Marine News' for June 2009 claimed that this acquisition was agreed by the United Kingdom Treasury so that the ships could earn dollars on services out of the United States. Two of these Victories, *Maron* and *Myrmidon*, were nominally owned by China Mutual, while *Mentor* and *Memnon* were owned by Ocean Steamship Co. Ltd. *Polydorus* and *Polyphemus* were owned by the Dutch N.S.M.O. to take continuing advantage of trading rights with Java.

For the new joint venture with De La Rama and Seaco, three new ships originally ordered by Silver Line were acquired by Blue Funnel Line in 1950, being named *Ulysses*, *Teucer* (which became *Telamon* in 1960) and *Teiresias* (which became *Telemachus* in 1960).

By 1947 Silver Line was under new management, led by members of the Barraclough family, and the company's policy thereafter moved away from cargo liner services towards tramping work, hence the termination of their round-the-world joint service with Prince Line and sale of the three new buildings to Blue Funnel Line. Interestingly, the 1930-built *Silversandal* was sold in 1954 to Moller Line (UK) Ltd. and renamed *Blyth Trader* to join the recently purchased former Bank Line ships *Blyth Explorer* and *Blyth Navigator*.

The Silver Line ships were sold by Blue Funnel in 1971, *Memnon* of 1959 being among the vessels which temporarily replaced them on what was by then Blue Sea Line.

Priam, *Prometheus* and *Protesilaus*, all built in 1966 and 1967 for Blue Funnel Line's UK/Europe to Far East services, as well as their four sisters built for Glen Line, entered Blue Sea Line service in 1972 and Barber Blue Sea Line in 1974.

Three out of four new ships built in Japan, named *Menelaus*, *Memnon* and *Menestheus* (the exception was *Melampus*), entered Barber Blue Sea Line service in 1977, their names being prefixed *Barber* from 1980 until their withdrawal in 1984. These were followed by the ro-ro ships *Barber Priam*, *Barber Perseus* in 1979 and *Barber Hector* in 1984. All of the Blue Funnel Line and Seaco ships, and also the new ships contributed by Wilhelmsen from 1977 onwards, retained the funnel colours of their owning companies.

Barber Blue Sea Line was not a financial success for Blue Funnel (Ocean Transport and Trading plc), contributing to the Group's total withdrawal from shipping in 1989.

Barber Lines A/S (Wilhelmsen)
On the creation of Barber Blue Sea Line in 1974, Wilhelmsen were operating the following on Barber Lines A/S services to the Far East and Middle East: *Themis*, *Temeraire*, *Tagaytay*, *Tai Ping*, *Traviata*, *Tarantel*, *Taronga*, *Tamerlane*, *Tirranna*, *Taiko*, *Taimyr*, *Talabot* and *Trinidad*.

Five new ships built in Japan entered service in 1977: *Tsu*, *Terrier*, *Tennessee*, *Thermopylae*, and *Talisman*. Their names were prefixed *Barber* from 1981 until their withdrawal between 1983 and 1985. They were followed by

Arriving at Vancouver in April 1981, *Barber Menelaus* was one of three ships built in Japan for Blue Funnel which entered Barber Blue Sea service in 1977. Their names were prefixed Barber in 1980 until withdrawal from the service and replacement by ro-ros. *Menelaus* was scrapped at Alang in 2001. *[Don Brown/Dave Salisbury collection]*

the ro-ros *Barber Toba*, *Barber Taif* and *Barber Tønsberg* in 1979 with *Barber Tampa* and *Barber Texas* added in 1984.

Conclusion

It may be concluded that the well-connected Barber Steamship liner agency business in the United States was more successful than the shipping lines which took on the risks of ship ownership in the twentieth century.

The name of Barber Lines disappeared in 1989 when Wilhelmsen merged under its own name three independent services into a single, round-the-world, ro-ro liner service. This survived until 2004 while Barber Ship Management became Wilhelmsen Ship Management. The Barber name last existed only as the first three letters of Barwil Agencies.

This history is dedicated to the managers and staff of Barber Lines A/S, such as Senior Director Kaare Isaksen, West Africa Trade Manager Konrad Ledsten, Ship Operations and Logistics Manager Tor Stensby and Chief Accountant Kjell Syversen, who had worked so hard for the company but lost their lives in a tragic aircraft crash during a charter trip from Oslo to Hamburg on 8th September 1989.

Wilhelmsen's *Terrier*, built at Tsu, Japan in 1977, which served Barber Lines until 1985, from 1981 as *Barber Terrier*, was photographed arriving at Durban in 1985 shortly before or after being briefly named *Hoegh Carrier*. The ship was sold in 1986 to the Chinese-Polish Joint Stock Company and renamed *Pokoj* as which she has only very recently been scrapped. *[Trevor Jones/Dave Salisbury collection]*

RECORD REVIEWS

LOOKING FOR THE SILVER LINING: A BRITISH FAMILY'S SHIPOWNING CENTURY 1875-1975
Martin Barraclough
A4 hardback, 352 pages.
Published by Bound Biographies at £25.00

The reviewer admits to a prior interest in this book. In 2008 the author enquired whether Ships in Focus would care to publish his work. Our answer was a definite yes, although we made it clear that the book would have to take its place in a queue and we would wish the fleet list to be in our own format. The author rejected both conditions and went his own way. Given that we felt it was a story worth telling, we are obviously interested in what has emerged.

The author sets out to chronicle the Barraclough family's involvement in shipping. This began with his grandfather, Thomas Barraclough, joining the West Hartlepool Steam Navigation Company in the 1860s and eventually becoming the company's manager and a major investor in its ships. After the sale of this company's fleet, Barraclough continued in the partnership of Webster and Barraclough until his death in 1916. Although not continuing with the partnership, his sons did enter the shipping business in their own right. In the 1930s Barracloughs became involved with the Dene Steam Shipping Co. Ltd., taking control in 1945. The book's narrative is now much more detailed, as financial records of this significant company and family reminiscences become available, although the reader interested purely in the shipping business may choose to skip much of the details of purely family matters. Involvement with Silver Line began in the 1930s with Henry Barraclough's appointment to its board on behalf of the Treasury, which had loaned the company money for new ships. The Silver Line story occupies over half the book, reflecting author Martin Barraclough's recruitment to the company in 1958 and his rise to Managing Director of Silver Industrial Holdings. This section in particular provides many useful insights into the industry, including the building and operation of conventional tramps, car carriers, ore carriers, bulk carriers and chemical tankers. Silver Chemical Tankers Ltd. and the rather ill-starred Seabridge Consortium receive particularly extensive treatment given the author's close involvement with both. To his credit, the author does not confine himself to the period of Barraclough involvement. He tells the whole story of Dene and Silver from their foundation through to absorbtion into the Vlasov Group in 1974. In the process he offers many revealing insights into the shipping and shipbuilding industries of the period and the personalities of some of those with whom he worked.

Visual impressions of the book are mixed. It is a handsomely bound book with a dust jacket which is a luxury these days. But although good quality paper has been chosen, reproduction of the black and white photographs is often poor. This is almost certainly down to the scanning or choice of original print, as a few photos have reproduced well.

The fleet list is lengthy and appears fairly thorough, no doubt thanks to the involvement of David Burrell and Bert Spaldin, although at least one early Silver vessel has been missed. The author's summary rejection of a conventional format for the list is puzzling as all the usual information is here, but very sparsely punctuated and in a somewhat strange order, with the launch date at the end as if it were an afterthought. The fleet list cries out to be interspersed with photographs of at least some of the ships mentioned. Surely including some here would have been better than the monotonous full page photographs of company worthies and poor reproductions of tedious newspaper accounts of launches? Books like this – especially those with fleet lists – are as much as anything reference sources, so the omission of an index is a major shortcoming, making it difficult to locate the numerous individual persons, ships and companies mentioned.

The author writes well and has a fund of knowledge of the shipping industry and its personalties which he imparts readably. However, proof reading is not an obvious strength, and he falls into the trap of making sweeping statements without checking them. For instance, on page 175 the *Silverbriar* and *Silverplane* which became *Andria* and *Alsatia* are described as 'the only second-hand ships to have been bought by Cunard'. A glance at a Cunard fleet list would show there were many earlier second-hand acquisitions, mostly freighters but notably the *Berengaria*. This reviewer often wished that details such as tonnage, horsepower and fates of the ships after leaving Barraclough's ownership had been left to the fleet list rather than be allowed to get in the way of the narrative.

With hindsight, it is probably as well that Ships in Focus did not work with Martin Barraclough: we would almost certainly have fallen out over what to include and exclude. It must be said that 'Looking for the Silver Lining' tells a very worthwhile story, especially the major sections which cover Dene and Silver Lines, two concerns poorly documented by shipping historians. With the author's first-hand kmowledge of the latter organisation the book makes a substantial contribution to the post-war history of shipping and shipbuilding businesses. The involvement of a forceful editor and publisher to enhance both narrative and presentation would have made what is essentially a good book into an outstanding one. It is definitely worth having, especially at the very reasonable cover price (which Ships in Focus could not have matched!).

Roy Fenton

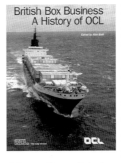

BRITISH BOX BUSINESS: A HISTORY OF OCL
Editor Alan Bott
19 x 24.5cms hardback, 288 pages.
Published by SCARA, 2009 at £22.50

Most shipping historians (including this reviewer) have tended to view the British liner companies of the mid-1960s as dinosaurs heading inexorably towards extinction. While this verdict might be true with regard to their traditional businesses, this splendid book makes it abundantly clear that it was not the case for either their ability to innovate or their vision of the future. Overseas Containers Ltd. was established in 1965 as a consortium of four of the UK's largest and oldest shipping groups: P&O, the Ocean Steam

Ship Company, British and Commonwealth (the recently amalgamated Clan Line and Union-Castle Line) and Furness Withy. The four principals behind the scheme (agreed fittingly enough at Brook's Club in the West End of London) were all knights of the realm. The man appointed as the first Managing Director was a retired major-general and, most surprising of all, the scheme received strong political and financial backing from no less a person than Mrs Barbara Castle, the then Labour Transport Minister! Starting quite literally with a scheme drawn up on a single piece of paper, the new company had placed an order for six container ships by March 1967 and made its first sailing on 6th March 1969.

Commencing with one route between Europe and Australia, OCL grew to become the largest player in an increasingly competitive industry, with a route network encompassing the globe. Existing agency arrangements and conference agreements were adapted as required, a complex series of new joint ventures put in place and, most important of all, the company did most of the pioneering work in establishing containerisation as a completely integrated process in which the ships themselves were only the middle part of a seamless movement of freight of all varieties. The founding partners had to overcome a whole series of organizational, political and technical obstacles along the way. They had also to deal with at times un-cooperative unions (the maiden sailing of the *Encounter Bay* took place from Rotterdam rather than Tilbury because of union action in Britain), two oil crises, the closure of the Suez Canal, and at times very grim economic conditions at home and abroad. Momentum, however, was maintained in the face of mounting competition from new entrants like Evergreen and rapidly-growing established firms like Maersk and, although the company lost its place at the top, it was still very much a viable and profitable business as it entered the new millennium. The original partners fell away – Furness Withy through take-over, and British and Commonwealth through diversification away from shipping – and in 1986 the company became P&O Containers Ltd. when Ocean was bought out, but P&OCL entered the P&O/Nedlloyd joint venture in 2004 very much as an equal partner. The new entity, however, enjoyed only a year of independent existence. The joint challenges of scale and stock market pressure left the management with little choice but to recommend that shareholders accept an offer from Maersk. It was globalisation rather than any company failing which took the box-boats away from the British flag – and it remains a credit to the original owners that their creation was integrated smoothly into the huge A.P. Moller-Maersk Group.

The fairest judgement on this book is that it should be required reading for anybody interested in the development of liner shipping over the last half century. This is not simply a tale of ships and men as so many company histories are – it covers every aspect of financial and operational management in painstaking detail. A large part of its value lies in its coverage of the development of containerisation itself – a highly technical subject which the authors explain both clearly and concisely. The book is also extremely useful for its coverage of the manner in which the existing shipping conference system mutated during the container revolution, and how individual alliances evolved or dissolved under the multiple pressures of fluctuating freight rates, changing political circumstances and new legal challenges. In fact, it could usefully serve as a condensed history of a worldwide business on the road to globalisation.

The book itself has been written, annotated, illustrated and produced to the highest standards. The collection of illustrations is excellent, ranging from colour photographs to contemporary cartoons; the footnotes and appendices are full of useful supplementary information, and readers are unlikely to notice that they are reading the prose of more than ten different contributors. Not the least of the book's merits are its heavy use of primary sources from within the company's own archives, and the fact that the authors were personally acquainted with most of the major protagonists.

This is such a fine book that the reviewer feels rather churlish coming up with a few caveats, but even these are fairly minor. The ships, which were at the end of the day always the most vital part of the business, do not really get the coverage they deserve. Major design issues are dealt with, but the book would be even better if a short chapter had been devoted to the evolution of the box boat – an awful lot changed between the first sailing of the 1,578 TEU *Encounter Bay* in 1969 and delivery of the last group of 6,802 TEU monsters in 2001. Similarly, the fleet list is a bit on the austere side and would have benefited from a higher level of detail. Some readers might also find some of the text a bit hard-going simply because the authors have gone out of their way to give due credit to the contributions made by several generations of directors and managers. Beyond this, the only fault this reviewer can find is with the some of the rather terse photo captions – I worked out in the end that the ship pictured on pages 79 and 80 was the *Encounter Bay*, but that was only by referring back to the picture on page 78.

Nothing said in the previous paragraph should put any serious shipping historian off buying this book. The reviewer has rarely learned so much from so few pages, and the publishers deserve to make at least as good a return on this book as their peers did from OCL itself.

Malcolm Cooper

KELLY'S NAVY
By W.J. Harvey
A4 hardback, 128 pages.
Published by the World Ship Society Ltd. at £27.00
'Kelly's Navy', subtitled 'John Kelly Ltd.: a Group Fleet History' is the latest in the series of such A4 hardbacks published by the World Ship Society, a number also by the same author. The book details the careers of almost 200 owned 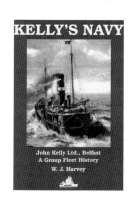 and managed coasters, plus a number of tugs and barges, illustrated by some 120 black and white photos.

As I did much original research 30 years ago into the family, business and ships, I opened this book with a strange sense perhaps akin to finding oneself back in a former house. It soon became obvious that this approach to Kelly does, in the modern parlance, 'what it says on the tin': it is indeed primarily a fleet history. The text narrating the firm's rise, heyday (it was one of the three or four most prominent British coastal ship owners in the 1920s and 1930s) and eventual gobbling up by ever-bigger corporate sharks, accounts for only about 16 of the 128 pages, something I thought was too thin to do the story justice, but to be fair the author does title this section 'company overview'. There are three random documents added as Appendices, which would have livened up the routine nature of this text: a war diary kept by Captain Barron of the *Crewhill*; a report by Captain Adair of the *Ballyhalbert* into a grounding near Ardrossan; and best of all a terrific personal memory of Captain Frederick Grant of Shoreham of a voyage entirely in fog from Antwerp to Preston, in his younger days in the *Carrickmore*.

'Kelly's Navy' therefore centres round the long and conscientiously detailed fleet list. I was especially interested to see the *Paragon* (409/1889) included, owned for just five months, and often alluded to as a possible fleet member by Kelly enthusiasts. Steamers ordered by Kelly in 1919 on behalf of the Irish Packing Company, a firm in which they had a stake, are also included. There might be a case for including the *Constance* (209/1906), briefly owned as a personal venture by Kelly's long-serving Marine Superintendent William Clint. However, there are certainly two steamers which ought to appear, but whose management by Kelly only became apparent on the publication of 'Republican Internment and the Prison Ship *Argenta* 1922' by Denise Kleinrichert (Irish Academic Press, 2001) – a book which the author can be forgiven for not having consulted. The former Admiralty steamer *Lull* (97/1918) acted as a tender to the *Argenta* (3,343/1919). Sir Samuel Kelly was close to the corridors of power in the Unionist establishment which began governing the new state of Northern Ireland in 1921, and the book details his firm's involvement in aiding the Ministry of Home Affairs acquire the ex-US Shipping Board's wartime standard wooden cargo ship, converted to house Republican internees. Perhaps 'obscure' (unless you were incarcerated!) but nevertheless the *Argenta* and *Lull* show that it is prudent to anticipate that there may be additions to any fleet list. (It should be pointed out that Kelly's management of these vessels was purely of maritime considerations. Internment is still an inflammatory topic.)

This is quite an expensive book, a very expensive book for non-members of the W.S.S. I hope the Kelly steamers' compasses were calibrated more closely than the index and page numbers. But the major criticism I would have is the range and quality of the illustrations for this price, especially as the ships themselves are almost all the book dwells on. About 40 of the 120 or so are credited to William Darlow, a quayside enthusiast in Londonderry, where 30 were taken, resulting in obvious monotony. Mr. Darlow's camera didn't seem of the first rank, either. Kelly traded all around the British Isles and near Continent; surely a wider choice of scenes is out there? Views of the *Glenmaroon* at Carrig-y-Llam and the *Annagher* passing Waterford en route downstream from Fiddown (place not captioned) show what might have been. About 20 views are recognisable as Preston, location again not captioned, and once more tending towards sameness. I also did not understand how a great many of these photos, of which I have prints stamped on the back with the photographer and/or copyright holder's name, are credited to 'World Ship Society Photograph Library'. I wonder has the publisher heard the last of this? I even spotted an uncredited photo of the *Carnduff* apparently abstracted from a book of mine!

The quality of reproduction is disappointing. Comparison with my prints make me wonder, in this age when the better scanners will enhance an image, how this can be so in a book for which a price comparable to grander works is being charged? My 80-year-old print of the aforementioned *Annagher* passing Waterford has more clarity and life than the rather 'flat' version in 'Kelly's Navy' (she is blowing her steam whistle as she nears the swing bridge).

'Flat' in fact is a fair approximation of how I felt after the initial promise of re-visiting Kelly faded. If the reader wants facts about ships, it is fine (is that what the World Ship Society sees itself as primarily providing?) but the vigorous, salty life of the Kelly men is grievously missing. I remember tuning in at the company call-up time on a Marine Band radio. A skipper was slowly making his way southward through The Minch into a gale. He was reporting to Dudley Barry, the Shipping Manager:

'Aye, Mr. Barry, we're off Dubh Artach light, having a bit of a splash. Aye, we're just making about two knots, Mr. Barry…'

These skippers were the heirs of the Ulsterman Captain MacWhirr with whom Conrad sailed and immortalised in 'Typhoon': laconic, maybe a bit dour, phlegmatic, respectful, immensely reliable and capable – men for all seasons at sea.

Ian Wilson

I write this note in my own right, as John Clarkson, photographer and photographic archivist, and not as the photographic editor of Ships in Focus 'Record.'

Normally I would not comment on books, being a firm believer in the saying 'those who live in glass houses should not throw stones' but for 'Kelly's Navy' this rule must be broken as I am so disappointed to see how poorly some of my photographs, and many others, have been reproduced. I had been looking forward to seeing the book, expecting to see many of Douglas Cochrane's photos but what did I find? Firstly, a large number of my own, as already mentioned poorly reproduced, with burnt-out skies and masts cropped. When I look at a picture of a ship I expect to see her from truck to waterline. One, the *Ballyhenry*, on page 73, is cropped at the top, bottom and right hand side for which there is no excuse: the entire ship is on the negative. The reproduction of the pictures is poor and if asked I would have supplied good scans. For this reason I am pleased they are not credited to me. Secondly, why use photos from my archives when the World Ship Society has a collection of coaster negatives, far better than mine, taken by the late Douglas Cochrane? Many would still have been taken at Preston but, 80 or 90 years on, beggars cannot be choosers. I am certain that if the author had shopped around he would have found good material taken in other situations such as at Avonmouth and Bristol, as there are many Kellys in the Bristol Series of plates. He may have had to part with some cash, or a few complimentary copies, but the exercise would have been well worth while. Thirdly, in regard to the photos from William Darlow's collection, it is always refreshing to see photographs taken by a different photographer in a different location but one must still consider each on its own merits. There are no details in the skies, some are distant views and some are not even sharp.

Is it not high time the World Ship Society appointed someone with a good all-round knowledge to edit and oversee publications at all stages of preparation and production?

John Clarkson.

A KELLY PORTFOLIO

These half-dozen views of Kellymen include two ships not illustrated in the WSS book 'Kelly's Navy', beginning with a wonderful view of the 1894-built *Cultra* (above), owned only from 1912 to 1914. Note the bridge, or rather the lack of one. The port is probably Bristol. *[Bristol Series, J. and M. Clarkson collection]*

The second *Corrib* of 1902 was photographed at Falmouth on 18th July 1931 (right). *[Ships in Focus]*

Carnalea passes Gravesend on 12th September 1932 (below). Completed in 1913, she spent an impressive 46 years with John Kelly or a subsidiary, being broken up as *Ballydougan* in 1959. *[J. and M. Clarkson collection]*

The Dutch-built *Chasmoor* of 1917 had lines similar to a typical British-built coaster (top). Bought by Kelly in 1931, she hit Bishop's Rock and sank in 1936. *[J. and M. Clarkson collection]*

Another long-lived collier was *Crewhill*, completed for Kelly in 1922 and scrapped as *Ballygally* in 1962. She was photographed at Torquay in April 1933 (middle). *[J. and M. Clarkson collection]*

*T*he motor collier era is represented by the brand new Goole-built *Ballygarvey* (2) running trials on the Humber in April 1982 (bottom). She became Stephenson Clarke's *Shoreham* in 1990. *[J. and M. Clarkson collection]*

A SHIP THAT MADE HISTORY

David Burrell

City of Everett passing Castle Island, Boston outbound on 30th November 1911 after being refitted for Standard Oil. See page 266 of 'Record' 31. *[Richard Hildebrand/Eric Johnson collection]*

On 21st July 1891 a strange steamer slipped into the Mersey, to catch the public eye and impact on ship design of the period.

The stranger was *Charles W. Wetmore*, the first whaleback steamer seen this side of the Atlantic. Launched from the West Superior, Wisconsin, yard of the American Steel Barge Company and completed in June, she loaded 72,000 bushels of grain at Duluth. Sailing on 11th June and passing Quebec on 28th June, she was in Liverpool for eight days during which she was open to public at a shilling a time (raising £115 for charity) before sailing for New York. There she loaded machinery for Tacoma, rounded Cape Horn and entered the North Pacific coal trade. Her end came on 8th September 1892, when, with coal from Tacoma for San Francisco, she stranded near Coos Bay, Oregon.

The brainchild of Captain Alexander MacDougall, the whaleback hull had an oval deck intended to allow seas to wash over without causing damage. Hatches took the form of plates screwed down to the deck, although problems were experienced with maintaining watertight joints and avoiding damage to cargo. The barge *101* was the first whaleback built, in 1888. Other barges and steamers followed during the next decade. Over forty were built, all but two by MacDougall's American Steel Barge Company on Lake Superior. The exceptions were *City of Everett* (2,556/1894) of 1894, built in Washington State and *Sagamore* from the yard of William Doxford and Sons Ltd.

Most whalebacks spent their lives on the Great Lakes. Last in service was *Frank Rockefeller* of 1896 which, as the tanker *Meteor,* became a museum in 1972. But *City of Everett* circumnavigated the world, and *Charles W. Wetmore* had a major impact on design. British designers looked carefully at her and went home to develop their own ideas. The most important outcome was the patented Doxford turret. Others included Ropner's trunk deck (see 'Record' 2 and 3) and Priestman's tower deck. The concepts of all three were similar, although detail differed to avoid patent infringement. An important feature of all was their natural self-trimming.

Sagamore.*[J. and M. Clarkson collection]*

Two deck views of the *Sagamore* which give a better idea of the lay-out of the deck fittings. *[Nigel Farrell; Ian J. Farquhar]*

Outside the United Kingdom there was Bredsdorff's patent, similar to Priestman's, and Alfred Christensen's patent oval ship (*Ekliptika*), a cross between the whaleback and Priestman.

The hatches were mounted on top of a trunk which was narrower than the lower hull. Where hull and trunk met a narrow harbour deck connected the two. In Doxford's *Sagamore* the connections to hull and trunk were radiused, in Ropner's it took a sharp 90 degree angle. In both designs the trunk was vertical, whereas Priestman's tower sloped inwards.

Doxford showed their preliminary designs for whalebacks and turrets to many, including Norddeutscher Lloyd; tanker owners Lane and MacAndrew; McIlwraith, McEachern and tramp owners like Jones, Price and Co.; Percy Jackson; Temperley and John Carlisle. Three preliminary letters of intent for whalebacks were received but two were not confirmed, a 4,700 deadweight for Runciman and a 2,200 deadweight for Gastaldi & Co, Genoa. The third, from Liverpool owners William Johnston and Co Ltd., entered the water as the 3,500 deadweight *Sagamore* in June 1893.

Doxfords encountered reluctance by owners to order these new concepts. To prove their confidence Doxfords, in partnership with Captain William Petersen, formed the Turret Steam Shipping Co. Ltd. in 1892 to own

and demonstrate the turrets. Similarly with *Sagamore*, the Belgian American Maritime Co. S.A. was incorporated in 1893 with Doxford and Johnston each holding 50% of the £5,000 capital. This company, renamed the Belgian Maritime Trading Co. S.A. in 1897, also owned the three turrets built for Johnston, *Ashmore* (3,461/1896), *Noranmore* (5,640/1898) and *Beechmore* (3,314/1899). The company having achieved its purpose, Doxford sold their shares to Johnston at a profit of £10,000 in June 1900.

The reason these Johnston ships flew a foreign flag were differences between British and Belgian load line regulations, international agreement not yet having been reached. British regulations measured freeboard from the harbour deck, whereas the classification society Bureau Veritas and the Belgian rules made allowance for the turret or trunk. Hence they could load deeper with safety, the difference in deadweight being a worthwhile gain. The Belgian ensign was a welcome flag of convenience.

Sagamore traded for Johnston until 1911, then passed to Italian owners as *Solideo* and *Ilva* before coming to a premature end when sunk by *UC 69* in 1917. Considering the longevity of some of the Great Lakes whalebacks it would be interesting to know how long she might have survived had not the war intervened.

Sagamore approaching Bristol as the Italian-owned *Solideo,* perhaps soon after renaming as some letters from her old name are visible. This view and the one overleaf show the curvature of the deck. *[Nigel Farrell; Ships in Focus]*

CHARLES W. WETMORE

O.N 126745 1,399g 1,075n
265.0 x 38.0 x 24.0 feet.
C.2-cyl. by Samuel F. Hodge and Co.,
Detroit; 800 IHP.
6.1891: Completed by the American Steel
Barge Company, West Superior, Wisconsin
(Yard No. 112) for their own account as
CHARLES W. WETMORE.
1892: Sold to the Pacific Steel Barge Company
8.9.1892: Stranded on the North Spit, Coos
Bay Bar, Oregon whilst on a voyage from
Tacoma to San Francisco with a cargo of coal.

SAGAMORE

2,139g 1,379n 3,500d
311.0 x 38.2 x 25.2 feet.
T.3-cyl. by William Doxford and Sons Ltd.,
Sunderland; 1,320 IHP.
15.6.1893: Launched by William Doxford
and Sons Ltd., Sunderland (Yard No. 215).
9.1893: Completed for the Belgian
American Maritime Co. S.A., Antwerp,
Belgium (William Johnston and Co. Ltd.,
Liverpool, managers) as SAGAMORE.
1897: Owners renamed Belgian Maritime
Trading Co. S.A.
1911: Sold to Cognati Schiaffino, Genoa,
Italy and renamed SOLIDEO.
1914: Sold to Filippo Bertoloto, Genoa.
1916: Sold to S.A. Ilva, Genoa and renamed
ILVA.
4.5.1917: Captured by the German
submarine U 61 and sunk by bombs, five
miles from Isla Colleira, north west of
Spain whilst on a voyage from Genoa to
Barry.

Solideo. [Ships in Focus]

Ekliptika at Bristol. [Johnsen, Oslo/Uwe Detlefsen collection]

EKLIPTIKA

2,167gt 1,348n
289.5 x 38.8 x 20.2 feet.
T.3-cyl. by Flensburger Schiffsbau
Gesellschaft, Flensburg, Germany; 900
IHP,11.5 knots.
6.5.1897: Ran trials on completion by
Flensburger Schiffsbau Gesellschaft,
Flensburg (Yard No. 166) for D/S Urania
(A. Christensen, manager), Copenhagen,
Denmark as EKLIPTIKA.
23.2.1914: Foundered in the Bay of Biscay
whilst on a voyage from the Tyne to
Cagliari, with a cargo of coal.

BOSUN'S LOCKER

When laying out 'Record' as with any other similar publication it is always difficult to guess what space there will be available for 'Bosun's Locker'. A week ago we had eight pages to fill so 'A ship that made history' was added, then a two page article came to hand and a further page went to Barbers. The 'Bosun's Locker' which had looked like being four pages was now down to two. No problem one might say, but at the time of writing this we are still trying to locate a photo of the *Ekliptika* for the previous page so we may have a further half page.

No matter how hard one tries when searching for illustrations at least one arrives on my desk just too late to use. The photo of *Uniceb*, the former *Benlawers* (4) on page 37 is a good example although it was intended for 'Ben Line' and not for 'Record'. Yesterday it happened again, a good view of the tanker *Felipes* arrived by e-mail. Too late to fit into the article but not too late to include.

Before giving details of the replies sent in about the photos shown in 'Record' 44 we have some good news and three obituaries.

MBE for Arthur Credland

Although having doubts about the United Kingdom's honours system, we are pleased to congratulate one-time Ships in Focus author Arthur Credland on being awarded an MBE in the New Year Honours List. Arthur was the Keeper of the Maritime Museum at Hull until

Felipes in October, 1958 being transferred from the Dutch to British flag in the Keppel Harbour dry dock at Singapore [Captain M. Pryce collection]

his retirement just over a year ago. He supervised the move of the maritime collection at Hull from a small museum in Pickering Park into the new Town Docks Museum over 30 years ago. He ran that museum, which later became the Hull Maritime Museum, virtually single-handed, with the assistance of the museum attendants and a part-time secretary. In spite of this workload, Arthur has written indefatigably, and we were pleased to publish his co-authored 'Bailey and Leetham' in 2002. Thanks to George Robinson and his 'Riversea' members for alerting us to Arthur's award.

Obituaries: George Scott and John Hill

Within a few weeks of each other, in November 2009, two ship enthusiasts well known to 'Record' readers died. George Scott and John Hill were always quick to point out that their interest in ships stemmed from their boyhood wanderings around the docks and quaysides of the River Tyne in the 'thirties. Beyond then, however, the knowledge which they were always ready to impart to others came from totally different perspectives. George remained a 'landlubber' working in local government and using personal observation from those same vantage points, allied to meticulous inspection of his massive collection of ship photographs, all annotated to record subsequent history, to become a renowned expert in ship identification. His speciality was cargo ships, especially Tyneside-built or owned, and it was rare that even the poorest print did not produce a positive answer for those seeking information.

John Hill chose the sea for his career, and his progression through the engine room was to take him to technical control of ships in the fleet of Furness Withy and particularly their Houlder Brothers subsidiary. The world-wide travel this entailed, and a vast library of shipping books, was to become the source of his further knowledge, freely passed on to others through his letters to most shipping magazines, indeed few articles in 'Record' could be said to be complete without the additional information he supplied, no matter what the topic of discussion might be! George Scott's public face was, perhaps, more discreet. His contribution to the world of ship research coming, in the main, from his ability, and willingness, to provide illustrations to book and magazine publishers from his collection, and identified only in the small print of the acknowledgements page.

George and John will be sadly missed, their passing in some ways marking the end of an era as that basis for their interest, and that of many more of us who have enjoyed wandering around docks and harbours soaking up everything to be seen, is denied by the stringent security restrictions now being enforced.

John Lingwood

Obituary: Keith Byass

It is with great regret that I report the passing in November 2009 of Keith Byass, family man, ship photographer and photographic printer. He was just short of 89 years of age.

Keith was a Yorkshireman through and through. He was born on and grew up on the family farm near Bridlington. After war service, mainly in India, he married his beloved Cynthia and they settled in Bingley where they raised a family of two daughters, Pat and Julie, and a son, Ian. In turn they provided mum and dad with five grandchildren.

Whilst working on his father's farm Keith studied art at Bridlington College and this led on to an interest in photography. Although he did well he went into engineering. Later in his career he became a representative, selling car tyres and continued with this until his retirement.

On one occasion his young son Ian asked his dad to take him to Liverpool to have a look at the ships. This was Keith's initiation into ships and ship photography. From there his interest grew, first just taking photos, then printing them himself and finally selling his prints to others. Selling car tyres took him all over the country and he never missed an opportunity for a few ship photos. Later he took on the work of printing the photograph offers for the World Ship Society which he continued to the end of his life. In due course Ian went to sea.

I first met Keith at a World Ship Society annual general meeting. We were both selling photographs and soon struck up a friendship. After a while we started pooling our orders for photographic materials and chemicals, meeting up every two or three months to sort out the consignments of paper etc. After a few years rising petrol prices made this uneconomical and we both went back to placing individual orders. We then went our own way just meeting up occasionally for a cup of tea and a chat. Towards the end of his working life Keith again took up painting – ships mainly but also railways and aircraft along with the odd non-transport commission. He was an excellent artist and was always pleased to meet us and show off his latest works of art. Christmas always brought a card with his best picture of the year. The last time Marion and I saw Keith and Cynthia was a couple of years back. He still looked the same as when we first met, a good head of hair, fit as fiddle and still had his favourite breed of dog – King Charles spaniels.

Keith died as peacefully as he had lived. He got up for his breakfast, didn't feel so well and went back to bed. About eleven Cynthia went to see how he was and found he had died. His funeral service, taken by a member of the British Humanist Society, was held a few days later and he was then cremated.

His negative collection – about 10,000 strong, and nearly all of his own taking, with some acquired by exchange and the best of Docker's collection bought in the 1970s - has been left to the World Ship Society.

John Clarkson

Information on photographs shown in Record 44

44/02

Stephen Brophy, Ian Buxton, Steve Cracknell, Archie Munro and Jim Pottinger identify the upside-down ship in dry dock as the German battlecruiser *Derfflinger* in the former Admiralty Floating Dock 4 alongside Faslane Wharf. The clue is that she appears to be in a floating dock rather than a dry dock.

Of the many ships raised following the scuttling of the High Seas Fleet, it is the 12 capital ships that attract the most attention. The firm of Cox and Danks, who had never raised a ship before, salvaged the capital ships *Moltke* in 1927, *Seydlitz* in 1928, *Kaiser* in 1929, *Von der Tann* and *Hindenburg* in 1930 and *Prinzregent Luitpold* in 1931, as well as numerous destroyers and cruisers. Metal Industries then took over, raising *Bayern* in 1934, *Konig Albert* in 1935, *Kaiserin* in 1936, *Friedrich der Grosse* in 1937, *Grosser Kurfurst* in 1938 and *Derfflinger* on 25th July 1939 in 1939.

Hindenburg was salvaged upright whereas the rest of the dreadnoughts, having capsized, were brought to the surface upside down and all were towed to the Admiralty dry dock at Rosyth for scrapping. *Derfflinger* was the exception. With war imminent and the Rosyth dry docks back in Admiralty use, she remained afloat but upside down at Scapa throughout the war, moored alongside HMS *Iron Duke*. In 1946 Metal Industries bought the surplus Admiralty Floating Dock 4 so that *Derfflinger* could be lifted and broken up at their newly acquired Faslane yard. The battlecruiser arrived in the Clyde under tow on 12th September 1946. Following careful calculations as to how the load would be distributed, a team of six divers built up supporting timber blocks in the dock according to the 'bottom' shape (actually deck/superstructure) of *Derfflinger* before she was docked on 12th October. The photograph was probably taken at Faslane on 9th May 1947.

Stephen Brody points out that *Moltke* has a unique claim to fame. Following a row between the two pilots involved, they failed to notice that the Forth Bridge was looming up and that the tide had carried the tugs to one side of a supporting pier whilst *Moltke* was passing to the other side! The tow was quickly cast off, and upside down, out of control and engine-less, *Moltke* passed safely under the bridge.

Further information will be found in Ian Buxton's 'Metal Industries: Shipbreaking at Rosyth and Charlestown', in Ian's article on Admiralty Floating Docks in the World Ship Society journal 'Warships' 160, and 'Jutland to Junkyard', published in 1973. Thanks also to Angus Brown.

44/03
Both Christy Machale and Captain Stephen Carter were quick to identify the tug towing the floating dock as the *Blackcock* built in 1886 by Lairds in Birkenhead in 1886 for the Liverpool Screw Towing and Lighterage Company. She was one of the biggest tugs of her day with a triple expansion engine of 1,200 IHP and dimensions of 146 x 21x 10 feet and a gross tonnage of 254. Stephen speculates what bollard pull and horse power would be required to undertake a sea tow of the same dock today. He thinks that with a single tug of 1,200 horsepower underwriters and classification surveyors would suffer from a severe attack of apoplexy.

Christy points out that a very similar photograph appears on page 438 of the December 1963 edition of 'Sea Breezes' (which also features a lovely study of the *Blackcock*, broadside-on from starboard, on page 432), and also, much better reproduced, on page 68 of Tim Nicholson's 'Take the Strain' (Alexandra Towing, 1990).

Ian Farquhar has submitted the above photograph, taken by the US Coast Guard on 7th August 1942 of what appears to be a MAC ship at anchor. The photo is marked *Mauna Kea* - Br, but Ian has been unable to find a ship of this name to fit the bill. Has anyone any ideas?

Bill Schell recently bought this negative of a sunken Liberty. From the other negatives that were offered with it, he surmises that it was taken by a US service man returning home by ship from Europe, perhaps around 1947. Assuming it was taken with a standard lens, the wreck is close to a deep, navigable channel. The background may help: your editors guess it might be a French port. If the location can be identified, it should be possible to name the Liberty.